the
voices
of
school

the
voices
of
school

*educational issues through
personal accounts*

Thomas J. Cottle

little, brown and company
boston

Library of Congress Catalog Card No. 72-12235

First printing

Published simultaneously in Canada
by Little, Brown & Company (Canada) Limited

Printed in the United States of America

The author gratefully acknowledges permission to reprint sections of his
book which originally appeared in other publications:

"Playing, Drawing, and Other Children's Foods" is based on an article
which previously appeared in "The Neglected Years: Early Childhood,"
published by the United Nations Children's Fund, January, 1973. The
section on children drawing is based on an article that appeared in LIFE,
December 17, 1971, pp. 52–53.

"The Other World of Baby Eyes Ellison" from the *Boston Sunday Globe Magazine,* September 17, 1972.

"Leo's Child in the Age of Aquarius" from *Time's Children: Impressions of Youth* by Thomas J. Cottle, published by Little, Brown and Company.

"The Golden Opportunity" from *The Urban Review,* a bimonthly publication of the Center for Urban Education.

"The Integration of Harry Benjamin," copyright © 1972 by Thomas J. Cottle, originally appeared in *The New York Times Magazine,* April 23, 1972.

"Schools and the Movie of the Mind," copyright © 1971 by Thomas J. Cottle. Originally appeared as "Car Shop" in *Saturday Review,* June 19, 1971.

"We're Born Dumb Hillbillies" originally appeared as "The Edge of the I.Q. Storm" in *Saturday Review of Science,* April 15, 1972. Copyright 1972 Saturday Review, Inc.

"City Teacher" originally appeared in *Saturday Review of Education,* December, 1972. Copyright 1972 Saturday Review, Inc. Used with permission of the publisher.

"The Chicanos' Run to Freedom" from *Change* Magazine, NBW Tower, New Rochelle, N.Y.; Vol. 4/No. 1/Feb. 1972.

Four articles also appeared in *The Prospect of Youth: Contexts for Sociological Inquiry,* published by Little, Brown and Company: "Harry Benjamin," which is Chapter 7, "The Integration of Harry Benjamin"; and "Child of the Land," "Car Shop," and "Wind" which comprise Chapter 8, "Schools and the Movie of the Mind."

To the memory of
Jack J. Weinstock
and Fan Hornstein

acknowledgments

I would like to thank first Leslie Dunbar and the Field Foundation who have helped so much in making my research possible — also, the Education Research Center and the Medical Department of the Massachusetts Institute of Technology. Let me thank, too, the following people: Kay M. Cottle, Robert Coles, David Riesman, George W. Bonham, Edwin Kiester, James Cass, Colin Greer, Peter Schrag, Robert Melson, Ernest Lockridge, Gerald M. Platt, Judah Schwartz, Jerrold Zacharias, Jacob W. Getzels, David Gottlieb, William Phillips, Joseph Lederer, Donald Cutler, Alfred L. Browne, Christopher Hunter, Freda Alexander, Helen Webber, Dudley Samoiloff, William Tobin, Mady Shumofsky, Harvey Shapiro, David Cudhea, Craig R. Eisendrath, Miriam Miller, Jill Hirshy, Eugene Lichtenstein, Benson R. Snyder, Merton J. Kahne, Robert Levey, Florence S. Ladd, Harvey Tilker, John A. Marvel, 2nd, Arnold Gallegos, and Oliver W. Holmes.

Finally, I wish to thank all of the young people, teachers, administrators, and parents, who were kind enough to speak with me and let their voices be heard in this book.

contents

the
voices
of
school

introduction

I have a young friend who lives in Boston. Terry Bingham is thirteen and attends what he calls an "okay" school located six blocks from his home. For the past three years he and I have been meeting, watching each other grow, I suppose, and inspecting one another's styles and plans. In that we do not see each other regularly, there is always a bit of catching up to do.

"School's pounding along," Terry will say. "I'm still hanging in there, winning some, losing some, keeping my bad eye on mischief and my good eye on college." Then he will pause. "And what you got to say for yourself?"

"Well," I will answer, as I did recently, "looks like I'll be writing that book on education."

"All those kids?"

"All those kids."

"Together in one book?" he asked incredulously.

"I'm going to try, Terry."

"Man, you got to be out of your mind thinking you can get all those kids together in one book."

"That may be, but I'm still going to try."

"Well," he said, "I want to see the way you're going to begin."

"You want to know something?" I answered. "So do I."
He laughed. We both laughed. Then he became serious.

For a moment he began to resemble some business people I know.

"Let's see now, who you writing it for?"

I was surprised. "Students, teachers, people studying to become teachers, parents, everyone, really," I responded.

"Everyone," he mused. "Everyone. Big seller like?"

"I doubt it quite seriously." He remained deep in thought. Then, as an idea came to him, he spoke.

"All right. You tell 'em that school isn't really buildings or anything like that, ball parks and swings, stuff like that. You tell 'em school's in your mind. In your head. Everything that you are is what school is. Like, school's happy or sad 'cause you're happy or sad, or it's big 'cause you're small or small 'cause you're big. You can tell 'em that. Tell 'em school's made up of everything in the world and that's why sometimes it's real cool, and sometimes it's the worst place any person would ever have to go to. Can you remember all I'm saying?"

"I'll do my best." I looked at him in amazement. He had one more thought.

"And since it's all about people, and since you ain't no television or movie man, you tell 'em that you're going to present 'em with the people who are in school, their voices like, what they're feeling, what's making 'em do what they do, go where they go. Stuff like that. Tell 'em to do what I do."

"Which is what, Terry?"

"Close my eyes every once in a while so I can hear all the voices around me. And in me." He had captivated me. "I can dig it," he went on, "'cept for one thing." He had already begun to laugh again.

"Yeah?" I wondered.

"You tell 'em to close their eyes to listen for the voices, you ain't going to have nobody reading your book!" He exploded with laughter, the top of his body bending forward, his hands coming to rest on his thighs.

I have introduced this book with the words of a young man not merely to show how a title was selected but, more importantly, because books on education, observations really of schools, students, and teachers, ultimately rest on the words and deeds of those people involved with school. It is the sound of voices that I have tried to reproduce in this book, voices that tell of a set of experiences with education. No doubt the pictures portrayed are incomplete. No doubt, too, my background and style of inquiry at times constrain the people with whom I speak. Yet, whatever the limitations of this work, one fact is always in evidence: Education is for people and about people. Buildings, facilities, regulations, philosophies, and techniques are the products of people. People's lives are awakened or dulled not exactly by educational methods but by the lives of other people. Culture, social structure, language, and personality may constitute the form of education, but its essence is found in the single life, in a single human being speaking about himself or herself, about history, circumstances, knowledge, and a sense of possibility.

Not especially self-centered, the visions and self-assessments I have heard in conversations with students, teachers, and administrators are as insightful as they are delicate. For at every moment these people are threatened by the power of politics, mass culture, and economic injustices. And still, education remains the one institution they continue to regard as the connection between childhood development and adult career and social position. Vocational training as well as learning for pure enjoyment remain prominent ideals for more families than one might expect. Human potential, talent, opportunity, and freedom are more than mere words. They are at the heart of what many people hope to enhance in the lives of those attending school.

So much, however, stands in the way of a human being maturing, learning about the world, growing with dignity and a conception of worth. To a certain extent, contemporary protest is lodged precisely because of these impediments. In the end, we want the dignity of people preserved, and their capacities honored. Yet, when some protest the existence of these impediments, others are frightened, and so they ask the protesters: "But you *do* want the best for your school and for your country? Surely you want this." But some protesters answer them, "No, that's not exactly what we want. We want the best for people. School pride is fine though at times troublesome. But what we seek is a school and eventually a world designed for people."

Because of the politics and economics that swirl about all schools and because of the sophistication derived in part from a knowledge of the social sciences, the task of being a participant in education is as difficult as it ever has been. Even the child too young to attend nursery school is implicated in the changes and resistance to these changes occurring in American education. Also implicated are students, young adults preparing for careers in education, and still older persons firmly committed to teaching or administration. And adding to the complexity of it all is the media's often overly dramatic representation of education and the self-consciousness born from the hundreds of studies undertaken in schools everywhere as well as the pronouncements made from them.

As sensitive as we are to the issues of education, some of us continue to push notions and programs at such a pace and with such an impressive ideology seemingly supporting us that we often seem deaf to the voices that ultimately constitute school. Is there not time enough, I wonder, for these others to be heard? Does their status, perhaps, fail to earn them a hearing? Many people surely have touched us by what they have said about education. Yet, when I think about school, I am struck not by any special ideas, observations, philosophies, or theories but by the sounds of human beings: their orders and pleas, their anger and obedience, their crying, their silence.

I am struck, too, by the fact that no one with whom I have spoken has described educational experiences that perfectly coincide with my own. Accordingly, we constantly teach one another what our respective educational histories have meant, and someday might mean. Strangely, though, I cannot rid my mind of the expression that goes: Under the skin we are all the same. A part of me wants to believe this, but even brief conversations in schools have convinced me that frequently quite the opposite is true. For when one enters classrooms one observes a group of young people acting very much alike. While clearly they look different, an attitude or behavioral style exists that makes them resemble one another. But when the class bell rings and they move in the halls, and I with them am flung about in a wave of energy and motion, even the traces of conversation tell of the differences, the qualities that proclaim our separate identities.

I would stress this singularity, although the perception of it is hardly new, because it relates to several issues in education. First, it reminds us that students, teachers, and administrators dread being categorized and having, in this way, their humanity stripped away. Second, it reminds us that these same people who often find comfort in standardized behavior and proper decorum feel as well a need to bolt from certain demands or expectations if only to prove to themselves that they are free and independent. Each of us maintains a complex balance between conformity and autonomy. Frequently we desire to be like certain others, but we also wish to initiate styles and moods that make us different and distinct. We seek alternative ways of acting or speaking, even alternative schools, and although these new developments may liberate us, we soon find ourselves rearranging the balance of a new conformity and a new autonomy.

Third, this awareness of individuality reminds us of those people who continually want their voices heard politically. Like the rest of us, they are curious to know in what ways their schools, homes, families, and geographies are special and unique. They are curious, furthermore, about knowledge: what there is to be learned and how it feels to learn. It is only natural, therefore, that they should be especially attracted to education and the destiny of those who are committed to it.

Finally, the consciousness of individuality reminds us of the various ways one can choose to work in education. In my own case, I have spoken with students and teachers, deans and principals over long periods of time. I come to these people with no particular questions, and, admittedly, labor hard to dissipate my prejudgments and premonitions about them and their circumstances. All sorts of private thoughts, naturally, are evoked in me during these conversations, and for at least two reasons I have chosen to make some of them public. My own reflections and utterances demonstrate to these people that we share a mutual reality despite the inequality in our relationship. (That I interview them and write about them surely provides me with a certain advantage.) A fundamental process of education, moreover, is itself interactive. We are with other people: sometimes as teachers, sometimes as students, ideally as both. Further, we recount experiences for one another, hoping that these experiences will be affirmed and considered part of the educational enterprise.

Throughout my conversations I have tried to sustain the idea that no person can fully speak for another and that no series of discussions nor pieces of personal history constitute a complete history. Even the most intense personal examinations yield only fragments of someone's life. The young students, who sit before us and for whose attention we bid, guard experiences that no school environment or method of social science inquiry can ever fully engage. More generally, the study of human behavior is endless; always there is more; another facet, another year's experiences, another person, another feeling. Still, the fragments of lives that form our images of the experience of school point to the fundamental issues of education.

Let me say a word, then, about the people in this book and some of the educational issues that their accounts cause us to consider. The paragraphs that introduce each chapter will make clearer to the reader how I met these people and, more precisely, what issues pervaded my conversations with them.

Education has always meant learning and the shaping of behavior. Whatever a particular movement in education may suggest, the development of personality, social relationships, and the transmission of knowledge occupy central positions in education. Factors, therefore, that influence children's development — as, for example, their native talents and capacities, social backgrounds, relationships with family and friends — necessarily assume significance in any discussion of education. In this regard, many educators use the word *socialization* to describe the major purpose of school: that is, the training and preparation of students for adult roles and careers. Those interested in student socialization may find themselves concerned with issues of authority and obedience, personal maturity, responsibility, and with techniques for evaluating all forms of student behavior. They may also choose to study the effects of culture and society, and the development of personality and classroom learning. Values, norms, and rules that regulate private and public behavior, they would argue, are vital parts of education. But so, too, are the institutions of politics, economics, religion, and the family which influence student behavior and development.

No one involved with education, moreover, can overlook the process of learning: How does it occur? What facilitates or inhibits it? What is the role of teacher? What is the role of student? Cognitive operations and the notions of intelligence and creativity are as much a part of education as classroom dynamics, teacher-student relationships, and the meaning of schoolwork. It is not surprising, therefore, that we have developed all sorts of methods of testing these phenomena and incorporating the results of these tests in the educational process.

The various chapters of this book examine these biological, cultural, social, psychological, and cognitive aspects of education. They examine, too, the effects of social class, ethnicity, race, sex, age, and environment on the individual and on the learning process, as well as on ways of seeing this process. In addition, reverberations produced in the classroom and in the lives of students by political events, social change, and community reorganization are explored. In order to make this exploration, students, teachers, and administrators from very poor, middle-class, and upper-class communities are represented in this book. Several American communities have been selected as the sites for the observational studies; some are in large cities, some in affluent suburbs, some in small rural communities, some in communities where English is rarely spoken.

The book commences with children too young yet to attend school, those about to become involved with a burgeoning preschool movement. It progresses through studies of various age groups, and concludes with those heading for high school and beyond. It considers issues of vocational training as well as of college preparation. It considers the social and political structure of schools, their relationship to local communities and to the nation, the rights and duties of teachers, and the experience of learning inside and outside the classroom, in homes and streets. Finally, it explores the personal development of young men and women, the public aspects of this development as well as the more intimate ones.

No doubt the reader will discover more issues than are listed either here or in the headnotes introducing each chapter. As everyone comes to the issues of education with his or her own perspectives and experiences, it is only natural that still more facets, more levels of richness, more limitations of education will be identified. Presumably, ideas for change will come to mind along with plans for what one would do if it were possible to relive school experiences or, better, to assume the role of teacher or administrator. But let me hope that no one's visions or designs will totally drown out the voices that constitute the chapters in this volume.

The Voices of School is not a book about groups of human beings or organized educational, political, or social movements. The people about whom I have written are experiencing that special balance between autonomy and conformity. At times, they seem quick to ally themselves with their brothers and sisters; at times they seek to be alone and unencumbered by the values and ideologies of institutions and of these same brothers and sisters. At some point, each of these people has evidenced a self-consciousness about the fact that he or she may not be a good representative of a particular group. "That's how I feel," some will say. "Perhaps women [or blacks or Americans or young people] aren't supposed to admit this, but honestly, this is how I feel." And then they will go on to say something personal in ways that make it seem that they are defying anyone to take away this one personal part of them.

The need for autonomy, privacy, and private reflection is particularly important now in education. It is disturbing to think that any educational or therapeutic ideology or philosophy would oblige persons to believe things against their will or against their sense of what is right and truly their own. Elders bend our visions and affect our voices, but so too do contemporaries. I am continually impressed, therefore, by those who can express their feelings knowing full well that as an observer I may stand opposed to what they have said. For this and other reasons I am deeply thankful to the people who have spoken with me and allowed their voices to be made public. I have changed their names and enough of their surroundings in my descriptions to disguise their identities. I have tried as well to reveal enough of myself in these conversations so that the reader may learn of the stumbling blocks and blind spots and, also, get some sense of the reasons these people revealed certain bits of information or emotions while keeping other bits tucked away and out of sight. Perhaps, too, so that the reader may be able to follow the wise counsel of a thirteen-year-old man.

"Tell 'em to do what I do," Terry had said. "Close my eyes every once in a while so I can hear all the voices around me. And in me."

chapter one

playing, drawing, and other children's foods

human development, creativity, and the preschool child

On a warm March day in Boston, I visited a park and watched two- and three-year-old children playing. I never met these children, nor were they particularly interested in my presence there. Too young, naturally, for formal schooling, they were nonetheless learning a host of things that afternoon, both about themselves and about the nature of the social world in which they lived.

Chapter one stresses the importance of learning through play and imitation in a natural and informal setting. It stresses, too, the fact that because learning takes place at very early ages, children arrive at school with knowledge, information, and indeed sophistication about social roles and work. The question, then, is whether we as teachers can see what they are doing, hear their sounds, and thereby take advantage of their knowledge and awareness. Children playing in a park remind us, moreover, of the open classroom and preschool movements which are now vital aspects of contemporary education.

In all of these aspects, however, there is the danger of failing to give full attention to the child's individual learning needs. Indeed, we may be doing children a disservice by perpetuating such labels as *preschool*. Human development, after all, just like formal education, is predicated on day-by-day experiences which ultimately have value in their own right and own time. Preparation for later experiences and learning is an important part of education, but sometimes we seem so preoccupied with what a child might become, that we minimize what he or she is experiencing, feeling, and learning right now. Then, too, we are sometimes so preoccupied with children playing in a park that we forget those children who rarely leave their barely tenantable homes.

I sat for nearly three hours in the park near our home last Tuesday. It was a bright, clear day and the children from the neighborhood who had been forced indoors for two weeks by blizzards and freezing weather ran about on the cold ground excited to be in touch again with the outside. The behavior of these preschool age children was quite similar. They would run from the swings to the slide, then to the merry-go-round apparatus that spun them about, and then back again perhaps to the swings. Always there were children whose behavior most of the others followed. Always, too, there were quiet, reserved, indeed withdrawn children who might sit in the corner of the sandbox playing with some dirt or a plastic cup or spoon. Occasionally these children would look up as if to inspect the changes of people's places in the environment, but then they would look down again and resume their work. *Industrious* would be one of the words to characterize the children, both the physically active ones and those who sought solitude. But the difference between them, a difference so obvious we have all observed it, is that some children were running together while others, presumably, found a glory in aloneness and quiet individuality.

I wondered, seeing those in the sandbox or those walking slowly about in the corners of the park, whether the schools they would attend in two or three or ten years would allow them to remain as freely independent from their comrades as they presently were. Would this productive social chaos be condoned later on? Or would the children be obliged to join together, to become a clan or miniature professional association? Would the attitudes and imposing style of the stronger or more vociferous children lead them toward ends they might not seek out on their own, ends they might even find terrifying and destructive?

Across from the bench on which I sat, a steep metal sheet is erected which some of the children attempted to climb. It is in the shape of a trapezoid: one edge long, the other considerably shorter. The design makes it possible for the smaller children to ascend to the top of the sheet. For, although the slope of course remains constant, the distance to climb is less at one edge than at the other. It is a clever and thoughtfully designed piece of equipment, but it builds in competition, too, and makes evident relative shows of strength and courage. It bids one child to dare another. It tantalizes the children's ideas of comparison and of sizing up physically and socially — ideas that the children last Tuesday seemed to evince as part of their natural makeup. The little ones longed to climb where the bigger ones did, and reach the heights of the silver sheet. I could imagine the feelings of the child who, clearly unable to manage this ascent, looked up into the sun and quivered. Then he bolted away as though either this one activity were too perplexing, or because another idea struck him. Back to the swings he ran, and in an instant he was sailing up and back, increasing the size of the arc by pulling hard on the metal chain just as the downward motion of the swing began. All the while he yelled, "Look how I can push myself. Look at me pushing myself."

I was struck in watching these children how a sense of autonomy and of competence were precious commodities for them. To be able to perform a task alongside somebody else and still remain strictly on one's own, if that doesn't seem paradoxical, was the rule of the day. To master a particular action, like climbing the ladder leading to the landing perch of the highest slide, or swinging, or pushing oneself on the merry-go-round, actions that had once required the assistance of an adult, brought sensuous and hard-earned gratification. The word *doing* suddenly crossed my mind. How important it was for these children to be doing things: with their bodies or their minds or merely with another person.

Tempo, pacing, and self-regulation were also a part of this autonomy and competence pattern. How long a certain activity would hold a child's interest was a conspicuous aspect of tempo. More intriguing, however, was how quickly the children would become involved in an activity. How long would they study the activity, and, once immersed, how quickly would they pursue the task? There were those whose natural pace or tempo seemed accelerated. Almost impetuously they flung themselves into their work or play evidencing, it seemed to me, a determination that problems to be encountered would be resolved on the job, as it were. These children, apparently, would do what was necessary as the exigency arose. Other children moved more slowly and more thoughtfully. I could see them studying the problem, the contours and slope of the slide, for example. They appeared as miniature engineers scrutinizing the problems and hazards of the job. They were, in a sense, dealing not only with the spatial and cognitive problems of the scene, they were managing the dynamics of time as well. One could actually observe them attempting to reason, infer, and anticipate. And all of this required them to call forth from memory prior experiences and what these experiences had taught them about slides and falling bodies, momentum, force, and acceleration. Perhaps they were physicists rather than engineers.

There was much more to observe among these handsome two-, three-, and four-year-old children. Some, for example, spent an enormous amount of time talking. Even when no one was around to listen, they jabbered on. Undoubtedly they were practicing their words, learning new combinations, or trying out the rules of speech that children in that miraculous happening come to learn. Even more, they were communicating with themselves, consulting even. Communing with themselves through language might be a more exact description. Through their talking they were staying in touch with their private worlds — worlds they might not yet be able to speak about, but only speak to. And they were using language and work to construct bridges between the world they saw about them and the world beginning to form inside of them.

None of this should sound especially surprising. We have all watched children playing in a park and told ourselves that each step we see them take is an exploration of the self. We have seen children's impulsiveness and their growing capacity to control, their search for chaos as well as constraint, their driving temerity as well as their periodic diffidence. We hear their squeals, their crying, their tearful or angry demands for justice and a democratic ethos, and we bear witness to their inchoate totalitarianism. Still, fairness is an important concept to them. Maybe they are not physicists as much as judges or politicians.

We hear children laugh, too, and this is a more complicated phenomenon than we might think, for we love the sound of children giggling among themselves and shy away from interpretations of it. But laughter at this age means so many wonderful things in addition to its presence as a sign of pure delight. It means a sense of inner happiness. Whatever the child's recent experience may have been, the sense of enjoyment, the capacity for devilish mischievousness, and the sensation of pleasure remain as possibilities. A child that cannot laugh frightens us. We fear that perhaps some inner light may have gone out. The children on Tuesday could make one another laugh. They made me laugh, too, these carefree entertainers and clowns. Maybe children's excitement with clowns bespeaks an identification with colleagues who unselfconsciously exaggerate goofiness.

Something else about the children's laughter. To look at the world and have things strike you funny implies cognitive maturation and understanding. Incongruity, foolishness, shame, audacity, comedy, and ritual are but a few of the concepts that children must comprehend, if only intuitively, for something to strike them funny. Tickling, of course, will do it. So will certain unfortunate acts, like slipping on a banana peel. But imagine what is required in the form of psychological and cognitive development for a child to laugh at the sight or sound of something. Imagine, too, what an extraordinary event it is for children to amuse themselves. We hear the expression so often: "The child is amusing himself." Usually it means that the child does not need our attention. He is playing by himself and is able to pass the minutes without our guiding or stimulating him.

Amusement, then, is also part of autonomy and industry. It is another fragment of that self-initiated and self-perpetuated industry that we earlier observed. But to make himself laugh, sitting there on the swing or on the large red block near the sandbox, well, that is special. What has he just told himself? What has suddenly come forth that has amused him so that he is utterly delighted with the verbal and imagic products he himself has generated? I find myself looking about to see what it was the child witnessed that amuses him. There is nothing. Just the tennis courts, people reading, and the other children sprinkled about the cold grounds. The amused one has communicated with himself. He has unwittingly discovered an inner capacity that will now enlarge his sense of self, his perspective. I hope, as I look at him, that his discovery will make him like himself. I suspect that it will.

But now, as fast as the laughter came from out of the blue a moment ago, it has disappeared, and this precious little boy has found another part of nature to peruse. He now sits on the large red block inspecting a cut. A small bandage has fallen from his index finger, and the decision he must make is whether or not to replace the bandage. I watch him look at a woman seated near me, his mother presumably, and he rises. Then, no, he sits again, and works the bandage back onto his finger. He inspects his efforts. It looks fine. He kisses his finger, then jumps up and runs in the direction of the small slide. At first I thought him a philosopher, then a doctor or at least an army medic. In any case, he has encountered the feelings of dependence and independence.

So much has happened in these three hours. Walking home I attempt to sort out some of my observations. Later on I shall not think intensively about these children, for something presses me to stay away from analysis and interpretation. Why try to figure them out? Why not let them be? It is so clear what children need and so evident how important to them are these years before they enter institutions of formal education. Social, psychological, and cognitive development is taking place, and, without question, many of the supporting structures of their personalities are forming. Although growth will end only in their deaths, God willing years and years from now, one of the things they presently are doing in their play and in their seriousness, in their waking hours and in their sleeping hours when they learn from the experience of dreams, is preparing themselves for all the stages of their lives. Though they may not be able to make these associations, their behavior in the park tells me that all of them are dealing with that balance between individuality and collective organization. They are finding themselves, as well as each other, and learning how they each influence one another. Sometimes they are made to feel unhappy by the presence, even a hundred yards away, of children whom, on that day, they fear or dislike. But often, too, they receive pleasure to the point of ecstasy from the presence of a friend.

Behind and beyond the child's play is what we have come to call the formation of identity. Publicly, it seems to start with a name. Several children asked for the name of a child they presumably had not seen before. The name became a title, a statement that here is a space that I and only I can occupy. This is me, my self, and that is you, your self. (No one need remind us of the possessiveness of territory demonstrated by these junior agents of real estate.) Learning about oneself and one's ways is part of identity; so is laughing and the slew of cognitive operations that biological growth brings to children. Some of the children in the park on Tuesday heard new words. They will not use them at once, but now at least they know of the existence of these words. They know, too, that someone has invented words. And how the children were inventing. They invented, it seemed, cognitive operations that they could not have imagined two months ago, like a sentence. More words in one breath today, more ideas packed into one phrase. And with these more complex sentences and notions the children in the park were learning the fundamentals of symbolism and complex representation. Quite probably, too, they were learning something of what mathematics is all about.

There was also a social world to be created or at least settled upon that morning. I am thinking not only of the leaders and followers but of the arrangements of friendships and the establishment of mutuality. I am thinking of the freedom to explore competitive feelings as well as cooperative ones. What is more, these children, for whom the notion of school is contained only in the stories their older brothers and sisters tell, are learning about their own alternating feelings of competition and cooperation, uniqueness or "bestness" on the one hand, and conformity or just plain getting along on the other. And that autonomy of theirs, that unpredictable, oscillating current that drives them to work alongside their partners one minute, sharing everything from toys to parts of their own anatomies, but urges them the next minute to work on their own, protecting their bodies and possessions in such a way that no army of bandits could capture them.

Repeating what many have said, watching the children last Tuesday causes me to feel that all the qualities of humanity are found in the play and explorations of children. All the feelings, moods, and propensities for cognitive and behavioral action are right there. One sees, for example, religion in these preschoolers. Of course they would only laugh and look ashamed if a grown-up heard them say "Oh, God." No one should mistake such an exclamation for religious awareness. The form of religion children really entertain is the appeal to ritual, to mystical, magical, and idealized thinking. It is the desire to be able to control events and situations so large and compelling that they fall beyond the realm of adults. I may be reading too much into the running about of those park children, overidentifying with them, as some would say, but surely I saw them wrestling with notions of the transcendent, spiritual, and unexplainable.

Religion is in the minds of preschool children. It is in their souls, too. But it is a tender and vulnerable soul that presently hosts religion or its genes. We can exploit that vulnerability quite easily and cause religion to appear before the child in one and only one light. We can also kill religion or make it difficult for the child to retrieve it at some later time. Without doubt the park last Tuesday had its share of ministers and theologians.

I saw health and sickness in the park. That is, I saw children, barely aware of the medical sciences, examining themselves, diagnosing, and even treating themselves. I saw the dogmatism and assuredness as well as the befuddlement I have seen on the faces of grown-up doctors. Psychological health, too, occupied some of the children. There is a marvelous way young children scan their lives and their environment, worrying about how they feel, comprehending a mood, not comprehending a pain or inner hurt, but all the while coming into closer touch with the mechanisms and the mystery, the physiology and the religion they will permanently carry with them.

I think of morality as being related to health. The preschoolers last Tuesday seemed quite certain if not adamant about their definitions of morality. At least they evidenced that their prior experience with people and with situations of judgment and rightness and wrongness was standing them in good stead. Like young lawyers, they argued their cases, calling upon precedent and invoking protocol and law. In some instances, they ruled on the misdemeanors of their comrades, and then sentenced them. It is hardly amusing to think of small children as hardened judges, wardens, guards, or bounty hunters.

Will is an arm of morality, and most of the children revealed the presence of their mighty wills. Indeed it was the will that seemed to connect morality to autonomy. And let no one doubt the intensity of a child's will or the fact that a child well before entering anything resembling school has learned ways to manipulate his will. That the manipulations may cause him grief cannot be denied, but while I felt my own anger rising up when witnessing tantrums and displays of unbudgeable determination, I had to laugh, too, because the power of these little people was literally earthshaking. (I am sure my laughter was caused in part by the knowledge that these willful displays emanated from the souls of other people's children.) Most of these urgent moments of chaos could be managed, even socially condoned, by the other children, but when the chaos was sustained too long they took a stand and enunciated their criticisms. They were confused and bemused by the furious one. Finally they walked away somewhat disdainfully, righteous matadors turning their backs on a snorting bull now agonized to the point of madness.

The years before a child enters school are exquisitely valuable years. In our country, we continue to be concerned with this treasured block of time that once mainly the psychoanalysts studied. The child must not languish during these years, we argue, for look at the morality, the cognitive capacities, and the intellectual potential out there in the park. Let us not forget either the still minute but no less real social order and sense of culture that these children establish and then live within. Quite a sight, their autonomy and interdependencies. Quite a complex society we and they together structure. They have learned about relationships with chums and have incorporated as well the fluctuating cycles of the world inhabited by adults. Equally remarkable is that such subtle phenomena as taste or preference should erupt out of this social order, this demi-culture, and that the child himself should be aware of some of the connections between the social order he has constructed, agreed to, or just passively internalized, and the private inner world he is now discovering. This again is part of that sense of self and the awareness of criteria that allow the child to differentiate between a sense of self and his own unique self. Well, the park did in fact seem inhabited by a few philosophers and psychoanalysts.

It also seemed inhabited by some artists, or at least children who reminded me of some children only a few years older who had exposed in their drawings much of what these park children were revealing in their play.

We tend to believe there is something magical if not deeply religious about a child's drawings, the elusive tracings of his or her interior that lie before us in the form or formlessness of a picture, a smear, or a scribble. We seem to see emotions in these drawings, unprotected impulses, anger, adoration, defiance, persecution, sheer fantasy unbounded by reason and adult constraints. Whatever the content, the pictures that hang in our kindergarten rooms or on our refrigerator doors yield, we insist, a valuable insight.

In the beginning, we are enchanted by these gropings or by these expressions that make little sense but nonetheless say something to us. Then, a bit later on, we see recognizable shapes in the drawings, for the child has come to control certain techniques and has discovered how to represent on paper what he perceives as well as what he feels. A momentous shift in personal development has occurred as social reality comes to be recognized and appreciated. There is an urge to bring forth an expression that corresponds to people or to things so that others can recognize them. And so a house is drawn, smoke rises from a chimney, a face has eyes, arms at last have fingers if not hands, and bits of the child's emerging personality gleam in the true-to-life shapes that fill his drawings — for his imagination has been altered by a growing involvement with the world around him.

Yet, unaware of the fine patterns of this incredible process, we lament the passing of what we call creativity. As the more realistic pictures of mommy in her dress and daddy in his suit bulge in the portfolio, we feel that school has killed the child's spirit. We regret that he has lost that glow of childhood, that spark of creativity. But in truth, that spark was not creativity at all. It was rather unguarded expression, an explosion rather than a thoughtful manipulation of impulses. To be sure, children are creating when they play and dance and draw, but the act of artistic creativity requires techniques that allow one to control and shape expression. Creativity involves the capacity to work simultaneously with human impulses and aspects of external reality and to apply one's own imagination and impulses to reality through a means of expression such as drawing. The first drawings of early childhood are essentially an outpouring of impulses. In the next phase of a child's drawing, the representation of reality and an allegiance to detail become important. Still later, there can be a phase of what again appears to be pure spontaneity, but those who go through this phase will be able to speak about the meanings of their abstract renderings — as they were not in their kindergarten years — relating them to the world they see and the feelings they are beginning to comprehend. At about this time we may catch sight of the beginning of creativity, which may emerge at age six or not until age forty. Alone, none of these phases in the development of expression constitutes creativity, but all prepare for its emergence. So, as the drawings of children change from the amorphous to the specific, creativity has not passed them by. Instead, its foundation is being constructed.

Last year I regularly spent time drawing with a group of kindergarten children. This fall I went back to visit four of them who were now in first grade in the same school. They had not grown much in the year since I had seen them. A bit taller, maybe, but the same faces and the same eagerness to work with me. But, actually, there was a change from the year before: each of them carried a small box of art supplies, and one of the new tools, I noticed, was an eraser. I laid out paper for them on the long blond workbench. They sat on little chairs and I knelt on the floor believing we would all once again dig into the drawing process. We did not.

They were waiting for me to do something, so I drew some amorphous cloudlike shapes and held the paper high. "How's that?" I yelled with pride. "What is it?" Joshua asked. "Yucky," another muttered. "Yucky," they repeated over and over again. "That's like my baby sister draws," said Claudia. They had refused to honor me as an artist. I agreed with them about this. But, more important, they seemed to know this year what the paper should look like upon a drawing's completion. There was a prearranged form, an imagined outline or blueprint that one merely filled in. There was, in other words, a distinct and immutable reality for them to represent. The hilarious or magical symbols of the prior year had vanished, and a serious recording of shape and design had become characteristic of this year's work.

Around the table, four children worked, one with a felt pen, the others with pencils. They made corrections, unlike last year, and uttered such phrases as "That's not right," or "That's not any good," or "I'm going to start all over again." They watched one another's progress, looking as much at their colleagues' work as at their own. Comparison and mutual inspection had become part of the artistic enterprise.

More slowly this year, dutifully and reflectively, little hands drew recognizable images. People and buildings lay before us. A year ago no one could have recognized a thing, and requests for labels or descriptions yielded fumbling gestures or blank stares. This year, a thoughtfulness preceded the calling-forth process. "Look at this," they exclaimed. "Look at hers." "This is my daddy with his pipe." "This is where I live." "This is my dog," Claudia said. "It's not very good. I can't draw dogs good."

"That, my friend," I said to Jason, "is a beautiful drawing. A turtle, right?" "Yes," he answered with great seriousness. "Did you just imagine that turtle, Jason? Make it up in your head?" I asked. "No sir," he answered, his eyes remaining fixed first on his paper and then in succession on the others' drawings. "I have a picture of a turtle in my book at home." "Yesterday I made a turtle, too," Jennifer said. "Was it as handsome as this one?" I inquired. "It was much better than that!" she replied.

The outline of the turtle was indeed copied, a penciled reproduction of an image taken from memory. It was an exercise in representation and recognition, an exercise preparing the child for a total act of creativity. At present, the turtle was not so much an expression of feeling or perceiving as it was an indication of the child's competence in being able to organize and reproduce reality. In drawing a turtle, the act of creativity is not of primary significance. More important are the experiences of competence in drawing and the learning how to define oneself.

The drawing session lasted much longer than a year ago. Each child made several drawings, requesting additional paper politely. This year the drawings were smaller, although scale and proportion were disregarded. At one point I suggested that unused portions or the back side of paper might be utilized, but my idea was rejected. And this year as they drew, their heads bent closer to the paper as if the images of the outside had been recorded through their eyes and were now being transferred through them to the waiting spaces of the newsprint. Occasionally they would lean back in their seats to regard their creations.

Then, assessing what *had* to be done, they leaned forward to resume their work. This, too, was part of the process of laying a foundation for creativity. For although the creative act is not one in which there is total conscious control of technique, creativity does require an ability to start with certain ideas and to be able to assess and perhaps change goals and ideas as a work is in progress. Often, too, it requires one to be able to work without knowing where one's project is heading.

In the year of my separation from these children, they had grown far more than my knowledge and romantic construction of childhood at first allowed me to perceive. For their drawings told of a transformation from making sensory images come to pass on paper, to making sense of a person and an environment with still unsettled limits. The inner world where creativity lurks had not at all been silenced in my four young comrades. Rather, their feelings and perceptions were being focused on people and objects that stand outside the self but shape it nevertheless.

Creativity, of course, implies an expression of self. What we see in children's earliest drawings, as in their play, is an expression delivered from the inside, from an inner darkness, which is dropped on the outside as a snowflake falling on cold ground. It arrives and, in freedom, remains there, unmodified, an entity not requiring temporal sequence or recognizable content. Later, the same expression undergoes natural maturation, as thought processes become more complex and relations with others become more sophisticated. Children's art reveals the poignant but inevitable interactions between a single self, still unformed, and a social world, still uncomprehended. While the content of children's imaginations and expressions is always changing, the drive to create and establish something that is uniquely their own remains very much alive despite our fear that it may be slipping away.

But that was a year ago. Now, I was almost home, wondering how much I would forget of what I had seen in the park and just what of my own preschool years I might be able to recall. The word that stays with me from my childhood, and from the park, is *play*. Let them just be, let them just do, is what I imagine many teachers presently insist upon. The park is fenced off so no one need worry about danger. The fence itself provides a spatial subdivision which more than merely symbolizes constraint and boundary. So let them go at it, and let us intervene at *their* call and for reasons of *their* health and protection. *Play* is the magic word. So many children use the word that it must mean more than it would appear to on the surface. Freedom to find oneself, or to be oneself when alone or with another, freedom to determine one's pacing or comfortable tempo, or the style of one's involvement with learning and industry — these freedoms underlie the notion of play. There would seem to be no need to structure too much, for a child can turn a sandbox spoon into a chisel or a car or, sadly enough, a gun.

Funny, that I should forget such fundamental park ingredients as indignation, anger, and violence. Why do I wish to deny the fact that children know and experience anger and at times even thrive on it? We might believe that anger is unbecoming in a child, but, not to play with words, anger is most definitely part of the becoming quality of children, and hence they must be allowed to play with it as well. Without the play there is no chance for them to learn the sensations of anger or any of its social repercussions. Even more, the child must learn not to be, well, angered by his anger so that he forfeits that delicate capacity to control his life and not feel overcome. Children as policemen and as criminals; children as angels and revolutionaries.

From my observations in the park I was prepared to write on the absolute sacredness of the preschool years. Granted, many cultures work vigorously to train the preschool child for school. It is not by accident that those gorgeous years should be called preschool years. But they are more. They are preadolescent years, preadult years even, but most of all they are years unto themselves. They stand by themselves as a two-year-old stands by himself; hence we may do best to rid ourselves of the temptation to view these years simply developmentally, epigenetically, or in terms of what they imply for the future.

Can we not, therefore, attempt to change our orientations to time? Can we not say, perhaps, that there is a beautiful and substantial, though transitory, quality and purpose to every year, every month, and every moment? After all, we do live moment to moment, affected as much by chance and accident as by "predetermined" biological or sociological events. Do we then honor the child and society by stressing the preparative aspects of these preschool years, or do we, rather, glorify him and his culture by suggesting that each day is itself both a preparation and a totality? If we were to emphasize the totality idea, we might feel more at one with ourselves, with our time, and with our culture.

For a long while we have been ensnared by an ideology that argues for the development of personality essentially during the first few formative years. Now, in light of other philosophies and empirical discoveries, and in light of what we experience, some of us might fear that the preschool years would lose their significance if we came to believe too strongly in the significance of adolescent and adult experiences for the shaping of the personality. But the genuine importance of these early years is evidenced not by the fact that we are formed by the time we are two or three, but by the knowledge that growth and development, what is in a word living, goes on as long as the heart beats. And, ironically, an organism's heart beats well before we see its face, and can stop even before its death. The significance of the first few years of life is diminished by the label *preschool,* perhaps especially by that label. Surely there is more to these people's lives than thinking about school, or preparing for it, or becoming socialized or acculturated. Surely, too, there is more to our lives than getting a child set and outfitted for school.

Societies must see the value and utility of reconceptualizing the meaning of these early years. If a society is to possess a vitality and an honest commitment to freedom, that vitality and freedom will show in the play of children and in the perceptions and preconceptions of this play by the adults who observe it. Only alienation or mindless conformity can come from socialization processes virtually demanding that parents hitch their newborn to the rails of adult success, obedience, or outlandish forms of loyalty and worship.

I am not thinking only of the arts, literature, or politics where a certain degree of rebelliousness or outrage seems to make men and women greater. I am thinking, rather, of all people and all activities, and of the danger of believing that the course of life is settled so soon, and that the middle and end can be so readily predicted at the beginning. If institutions of education, and political, social, and economic systems will permit it, the day-by-day leading of a life can be *the* colossal creative act. It can be, moreover, the direct consequence of those early years of explorative play and discovery. My own inability to call up my earliest years, an inability caused in part by neurological and psychological impediments, suggests that a situation faced by us all is that childhood, history, and our personal and cultural antecedents are taken away from us. Thus we are obliged to lead our day-by-day lives as if our childhoods or child*like* ways were something to be shunned and forgotten.

The predisposition to examine childhood in purely preparative terms, like *preschool,* has an equally frightening mirror image. It is that we will be left to encounter the chances and predictables of life separated not only from our own histories as adults, but also from our propensities and destinies as children. This to me is quite a price to pay. A heart no longer as young and as seemingly indestructible as a child's heart might well be unable to sustain this load. And no society ultimately can afford to let its children develop into adults with these assumptions underlying the contract for living.

Nonetheless, the primacy of play would seem to be the central concept to come out of these observations. Play was at the center of the children's behavior and activities last Tuesday morning. Through play, a child develops a sense not merely of freedom, expression, and creativity too, but, ironically, a need to be constrained, or at least have his expressions defined. Play, therefore, is one of the first steps of personal and social evolution. It is a step of enunciation and of coming into contact with a world of seemingly endless possibility. One, presumably, can do anything because each human being carries the potential of an entire civilization. This is the way it should be. Constraints and restrictions are inevitable products of any society. Right or wrong, a child ultimately will be, as we say, toned down. But the child who has never known the experience of encountering his or her own potential is a child too early silenced.

Now we might believe that our various cultures are wise to get their children in line as soon as possible in order to assure well-mannered, well-appointed, and obedient citizens. But the result of the suppression of play is not necessarily an orderly citizenry or assured obedience. Instead, it can be alienation, people separated somehow from themselves, unaware of their own capacities, doubting their talents, and mocking their hopes. Play is a forerunner of work and creativity. It is more than an activity. It is a medium through which people mature and cultures are made richer, if not necessarily healthier. Through play, children come to learn their connections with the past and with the present world of their comrades and elders. Play is their own product, self-initiated and molded according to criteria children themselves establish and impose. Allowing children to play permits them to experience the necessity of both individual action and social control. It permits them, moreover, to experience the meaning of choice and from this the limitations set by any society, culture, or indeed by any person for himself.

Play is opportunity, the chance, well, to have a chance. To grow up wondering about one's capabilities most probably leads to a quiet inner sadness and sense of worthlessness. Through play, personal exploration, and an atmosphere of free choice, a person at least has the opportunity of discovering what he cannot do, or cannot do well enough so that he feels adequately gratified. Still, he has made his attempt and has come to know in his body as well as in his mind the feelings of that activity and that one venture. For many of us one time is sufficient. We know the activity is not for us, and this fact adds to our knowledge of what it is that we are and what it is that our biology and psychology and intellect have made possible for us.

Looked at from this perspective, play becomes a major activity in the shaping of a philosophy. Play will at least advise the child of the existence and worth of such a thing as a personal philosophy, and of its relationship to social ethics and cultural values. Paradoxically, then, play brings the child into contact with himself and with the dynamics of generations, customs, and rituals. Play provides a sense of continuity in that it teaches the inevitability of repeating and accumulating experiences as well as the inevitability of discontinuity, for change and innovation are the scions of play.

One could go on summarizing the values inherent in children's play behavior. But I believe that the qualities the park children revealed are best described as *imagination* and *autonomy*. Even as they ran about following or mimicking their temporary leaders, anyone could have seen that their capacity for imagination was practically limitless. Anything could be enacted in their minds. They could become anything or anyone; they could be creators of worlds that never existed (or so *we* imagine), children living free of any temporal order or spatial constraints. This means that someday they might conceive of and bring forth notions, products, or inventions that no one before them has even dreamed of. No culture survives without these products of imagination, albeit they will be transformed by adult intelligence, adult need, and adult forms of education.

Personal autonomy, self-possession, and integrity were also part of the play last Tuesday. Granted, children of this age continue to depend on one another and their elders. This we can easily observe. In their play, however, they were tasting independence, self-generated work, and personal actuation. Alone they commenced work, brought it to completion, and then stood back to see what they had achieved and what these moments of work and achievement felt like. Again that phrase appears: the child amusing himself, playing with God-given skills free of noticeable influence. This is the basis of learning, a basis that in no way precludes teachers but, instead, prepares for the entrance into the child's life of teachers and ultimately of the wisdom of other human beings.

Last Thursday I visited two homes in the southern end of Boston. In one home there were six children; in the other there were five. Several of the children in these homes were too young to go to school. It was cold in their homes, and the children were hungry, even though they had eaten something shortly before I arrived. It seemed quiet in these homes given the number of children. There was little movement; an irritable sense of confinement appeared to have overcome the children. They clustered around me, not at all like the children in the park two days before, and I felt as though they were wishing that I might change the current of their lives — or maybe just take them to visit the park near my home. I felt, too, that these children were older than I, closer to some end than I, and I wished that they would know what I felt in their presence.

I admit that I am uncomfortable in the neighborhoods of the poor. I often park my car several blocks from their homes in order to suggest that I ride public transportation. I cannot decide what to do when food is offered me, as it invariably is, because I know about budgeting and scarcity as much as I know about a desire to be a giving host. I cannot sit down on a chair or sofa without wondering whether my presence is legitimate.

I feel a shame that comes from my childhood, from my frequent incapacity to see and to hear what is before me so close at hand. It is a shame that comes, too, from leading my life in such a way, perhaps, that these eleven children cannot lead theirs as I would want them to, and a shame that comes from the knowledge that I have the right to sit in a park and watch free children play, and dream my dreams, and construct my arguments and concepts. These eleven are for sure "preschoolers," developing in their ways and with their capacities the very same human ingredients those other children were. The difference between the groups, however, is that society will not stand behind these eleven and support them, feed them, and care for them, or even arrange for the angels of chance to play their games. They are not forgotten children. No, indeed, they are very much on our minds and in our conversations. And this may be the supreme tragedy: that we keep them in our minds and in our conversations and inadvertently, or deliberately, refuse to let them play and grow underneath our skies.

chapter two

the
young
and
their
prophets

*peer groups, heroes,
and the reality of
street learning*

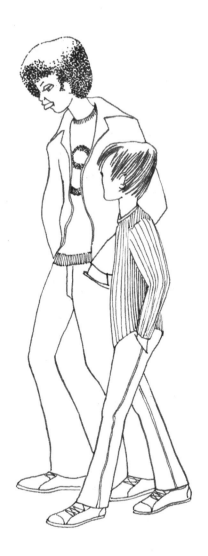

I met Rico Bartolini and Spider Wormsley along with several of their friends in the Dorchester area of Boston. They were playing ball one afternoon, and I happened to be in the neighborhood. One of their teachers introduced us, and we soon became friends.

What these young men have taught me is how much young people learn outside of school: in the streets, in one another's homes, and just walking around. Some of the most important learning experiences take place outside of schools. We know that contemporaries teach one another, but heroes are perhaps the most significant teachers because of the power and intensity they can generate in relationships with their followers and disciples. Such intensity is usually not possible in a normal school setting, and although teachers are aware of the shortcomings of classroom activities, they may not always remember the sorts of learning experiences that their students are going through after school, in the evenings, and on weekends. They may forget, too, as they undertake their teaching chores, that these youthful experiences are hardly extracurricular but in fact form the basis of a young person's adaptation to an adult world.

For Whip, Rico, Spider, Philly, the Taylor, and Spanish, the stories were remarkably similar. Six young men, about ten, eleven, and, in Spanish's case, thirteen, had all experienced the same thing; each had in fact known a leader, a prophet. There very well might be elaborate interpretations of this sort of experience. I myself had tried again and again to comprehend it, for those of us with some training in sociology tend to become especially interested, not in single events exactly, but in the curious repetitions of events. Four times I had heard of the same thing happening, and now with Rico and Spider I was catching the experience as it unfolded.

Rico's and Spider's experiences had taught me much about the nature of the involvement. When each was about eleven he found himself worshipping an older boy of about sixteen or seventeen. In Rico Bartolini's case, the worshipped one was Wendell Graves, a tall, strong, young man, a member of the high school basketball team, and a man with supreme inner strength that matched his showy style and beguiling manner. Both Rico and Spider were fatherless — a fact that later gained importance. Both longed for but trembled under the power of a strong man. At any rate, when Rico was about eleven he held Wendell in awe. The fact that Rico belonged to the Juniors, a neighborhood gang, and that Wendell served as the first vice-president of the Lords, the gang into which the Juniors would graduate, only enhanced the admiration that the younger one held for the older one.

Rico would follow Wendell everywhere, running errands for him, fetching things for him, and gradually getting caught up in Wendell's sexuality and thirst for hard drugs. When he was fifteen Rico told me: "Wendell used to tell me things like, 'Go over to Smitty's locker. The combination is, you know, something left, something right, something left. You'll find a little bag in there. Get it for me and I'll give you a quarter. You see a cop you run the other way. You hear me, boy?' Which I always did. He'd tell me too, 'Don't you go lookin' in that bag. I'll beat the shit out of you any moment I find out you've been poking around in it.' Or maybe it would be with a girl. Man, I remember once I had to go over to the project one night about ten o'clock. Wendell said he'd beat me if I didn't do this. I had to lie to my mother and everything to get out. She wouldn't let me go, so I sneaked out. Boy, did she pound me the next day when she discovered I'd been out. I sneaked back in through the fire escape but she'd checked on me while I was gone. Well, anyway, that time I had to go to this chick's house and deliver this message. Man, you should've seen this girl. Oo-ee, was she ever something. I told her something, must have been a code or something, and she got all excited and gave me this kiss on the cheek. She didn't know what I was thinking, but she sure was in a hurry to meet Wendell. Next day he told us all about what they did.

"I remember, a bunch of us were sitting around and Wendell was there. I used to think once in a while, I wonder what this guy's up to? Nah, that isn't right. That's kind of more what I think about now. I guess then I was so taken by the guy that I just used to think, man, what a good guy he was taking all this time away from being with kids his own age just to be with us shrimps."

"What did he tell you then, Rico?" I asked.

"Well, this is going to sound strange, I know, but you'll have to believe me."

I smiled. "I will. I promise you."

"Well, that's easy for you to say 'cause you ain't heard nothing yet."

"Go on. Try me."

"O.K. But remember, this is the truth. You ask Spider if it's not."

"Where is Spider?"

"I don't know. He said he'd meet us here." Rico, Spider, and I had planned to meet near the neighborhood park in Boston's South End. Spider had a job in a laundry and we hoped he might get away. Rico was between jobs, having just quit work in a restaurant because of his fear of the owner who threatened to beat him all the time, a threat that was exacerbated when I tried to intervene. He was presently hoping that a delivery job with a florist on Tremont Street might open up. He wouldn't know about this, however, for two weeks. In the interim, Rico ran the numbers to make the money his mother counted on his contributing to their family of six.

"Well, here goes. Shit. I hope Spider gets here soon."

"He will. Hey, Rico, maybe you'd just as soon forget this story. You don't have to tell it, you know. I've been pushing you a little hard."

"No, you haven't, man. Sometimes you do. The Taylor and me, we once thought about telling you to stick it up your ass when you asked us something once."

"Why didn't you?"

"We, ah, well, you know, you can't go tellin' some guy, especially an old dude like you, to stick it up his ass."

"I guess you're right, although you sure think of it often enough, don't you?"

"Right on." Rico smiled that beautiful smile of his. " 'Specially in school with the priests or those big-shot teachers or coaches or guidance counselors they got running your lives for you. They really think they can cast some spell over people our age. The same spell, I guess, that Wendell had. I guess I better tell you.

"See, it all began with some of us, like Spider and the Taylor thinking old Wendell was a pretty hot shit old guy. We watched him around, you know, here and there. We'd see him goin' to the movies or to the record store with some girl. Shit, we used to think he was really something else. Then he made the basketball team. Oh man, we'd run off and see them play. Hell, they even played once in the Garden. Same place the Celtics play. Down we went, man. Got lost, too." Rico laughed and shook his head from side to side. "Man, did we *ever* get lost. Big place, Boston. You need someone to show you around. First time, anyway. You need some guy who'll keep you from getting lost first time.

"Anyway, we got there and saw Wendell. He was really beautiful, man. Scored fifteen points. Six from the floor, I remember, the rest on free throws. He wasn't really the best, but Spider and the Taylor and I, we always said he was the best, like. And he'd have all these guys and girls goin' crazy every time he got the ball. Something about him. There was just something real special about him."

"Like what, Rico?"

"I don't know. One thing was that he was big. Man, he was big. Not just bigger than us, but big for his age, you know. He must have been six five."

"Really?"

"Oh, yeah. He was really a monster. But his voice was very quiet. That was the part I think about the most when I think about him. He was big and strong, and tough too. Even in basketball. He was strong, like a bear, but he had this quiet voice that sounded real nice when he spoke to you. At least it did to me. 'Course we were so small that if he ever said hello we'd just about go out of our heads. You know what I mean?"

"Yup. I sure do. Once I shook Robert Kennedy's hand and he said, 'Glad to see you,' in this quiet voice. It sure made me feel funny inside. Like I would have followed him anywhere."

"That's it, man. That's the thing I've been trying to tell you. Explain to you, I mean. I'd have followed Wendell. I did follow him, although I'm not so sure I would have if I had been by myself. The other guys, like Spider, if he ever gets here, they were part of it too."

"I know what you mean."

"Yeah. They're an important part. Like I remember seeing Wendell after the game. Even though they lost, everyone went down on the floor to see the players. Taylor and me, we just ran down like a bunch of mentals. 'Course it was exciting just walking on the same floor the Celts played on. You know, all these little squares and the little marks their shoes make. Boy, that was some feeling. You know?"

"Oh, yes." I remembered being a child and walking on the field where the Chicago Cubs played. The grass seemed so different from any other grass, and the contours of the field, the dips it made for drainage, contributed to the feeling that I was on a meadow connected to heaven itself. Something else about standing on Wrigley Field. There was an unobstructed view into the dugout, a perfectly open view of the bench where the players sat, the little hooks on which they hung their warm-up jackets, the water fountain from which they drank, and the cement floor on which their spikes clacked.

"Well," Rico was continuing, "we saw Wendell that day. He was all sweaty, and girls were all around so we thought he'd never see us. But damned if he didn't see us. 'Little Rico.' That's what he said. That's what he called me. Little Rico. I remember I waved and felt silly. All the girls looking at me, and here I was standin' in the middle of the Boston Garden. Shit, man. It was really a strange, spooky feeling. Like I was the only guy there, even though the place was filled up, I mean, filled up for a high school basketball tournament game. But when he said my name out loud, that was really out of sight, man."

"That sounds real nice. I mean, lots of us have experiences like that. Where we feel recognized, and all . . ."

"You wait."

"O.K. I'm waiting."

"When we got to know Wendell better, there were some guys we knew who warned us about him. They used to call him the Prophet. All spooky and everything."

"Why so?"

"I don't know. He was strange. Well, like this here. One night there were about five of us little guys, and Wendell, and a girl, and another guy on the team. I didn't know him. He flunked out or quit or something. Anyway, Wendell starts talking like we're in a church or something instead of just sitting on these benches outside. He's got his arm around his girl and they're all smoking and offering us cigarettes."

"You take one?" I looked at him.

"What you looking at, man?" he asked.

"You."

"Yeah? For what reason?" Rico began to smile.

"I'm just looking." I couldn't keep a straight face.

"You think I'm taking dope?"

"No."

"Hell you don't."

"I don't," I answered.

"Bull . . . shit." He stretched the word out as far as it would go.

"Bullshit nothing." I've always felt funny about swearing in front of boys like Rico, Spider, and the Taylor. It's not morality or even their age that constrains me. Anybody that spends time with a certain group of young people learns quickly the boundary lines of morality and decorum. No, I felt somehow that to appear straight would make them like me better. It was the way I chose to let them know my feelings that there were all sorts of boundary markers between them and me, and that all of us would have to extend ourselves to be close. Perhaps I didn't want to feel myself becoming indistinguishable from them, or them from me. Whatever the reasons, I always received a look when I would use an expression or swear or do something which they believed was not in keeping with my character.

"Rico, I don't think you're a dope head. Stop putting words into my mouth."

"Well, O.K." He smiled. " 'Course, I was before we met."

I laughed out loud. *"You're the monster,"* I said.

"You think so?" He sounded like a little boy.

"No, I'm teasing."

"Lots of people think I am, you know." He was deadly serious.

"No. I don't. I'm sorry I used the word."

"Lots of people think I'm pretty bad news."

"I don't."

"Well, O.K. But lots of people do."

I would come back to this, but not now. Not today probably. "Go on about Wendell."

He paused. "Let's see." Rico rubbed his forehead with his index finger. "Wendell, Wendell, Wendell. Oh, so anyway, we're there in the park smoking and Wendell's telling us how to, you know, be good guys. He's telling us how we shouldn't smoke or drink. And we should help our parents and our brothers and sisters. His girl is looking at him real strange. I remember that, 'cause I was kind of angry with her that she wasn't paying close attention to the Prophet. That's what we called him. And he told us what would happen to us if we got into trouble at school, or in the streets. You know. Thing was, you see, we were so young we were always messing around or hitting each other. Never listening half the time. But the Prophet, he'd play along with us and then kind of stick in his serious stuff when we'd get a little quieter. Like, he'd tell us about God. I remember he wanted us to believe in God. He used to tell us that the part of us that loves is the part that God gave us, and the part, like he used to say, of us that is God living inside of us. And then the bad parts were supposed to be the devil inside of us. Something like that. You know better than me. I forget now. But religion and all was very important to the Prophet. He was always acting like a minister to us. Someone said once that his old man was a minister, but he drank too much and died.

"That's another thing, I just remembered. The Prophet always said we had to lead a very clean life. No drinking, no smoking, or nothing. Then in the next minute he'd be giving us cigarettes, and finally one day he gave us some real wild stuff. Man, we didn't know what the hell it was. We just took it and everybody tried to tell each other what we were feeling. What got me about the Prophet was that even though I really dug him, and all, I mean he was really big and special to us, 'cause you know, like I never really had no father or older brother so anybody taller than me's already got the power where I walk. . . ."

"Even me, Rico?" I smiled at him. Rico was rather short but, as we were seated, our eyes were on the same level. He looked at me, measuring my height.

"Yup. Even you. When I'm with you, you got all the power."

"I interrupted you."

"Yeah, let's see. Oh, yeah. See, I was always scared somehow when the Prophet was around. I always felt that I had just better do whatever the man said 'cause if I didn't something bad would happen. Man, I wish Spider or the Taylor were here. They wouldn't say they were scared, I'll bet, but they were. Once we talked about it. They all said there was a spell the Prophet kind of let out, and if you got caught in the spell it was all over for you. Man, I wasn't scared. I was petrified. My heart would be beating so fast all the time. I'd be walking down the street and see some shadow and I'd panic. I'd think it was the Prophet coming to get me and take me somewhere."

"To do what with you?"

"Oh, I don't know, man. I don't think I ever let myself think about it. Maybe he'd take me in an alley and cut off my arms, or maybe he'd stick a big knife in my ribs. You know. Whoosh. And all the blood would be flying out all over the place."

"He really scared you, didn't he?"

"You ain't just kidding. I couldn't tell no one neither. Like the night with the dope. He made us sit very quietly on these benches. It was right out there in the middle of the park somewhere, man." Rico pointed in the direction of the window toward a park located more than five miles from where we now were speaking. "We all sat there waiting to do whatever he said. I remember I was wishing I was home and in my bed. All curled up under the covers, you know, like when it's real cold outside and you can get all warm inside the bed. So anyway, the Prophet he passes this stuff around and shows us how to breathe real deeply like so that we suck the dope way down in our lungs. You should've seen the Taylor." Rico began to laugh, his words coming out in between his gasps for breath. "You should've seen him, Tom. He was gagging and wheezing and we were laughing. Everyone. I was real scared even though I was laughing, and the Prophet he just stayed real mild like, and his same old serious way. He never changed. Wait 'til I tell you."

"Tell me what?"

"You'll see. Where's Spider? He's always late." Rico looked toward the window.

"He's probably working and can't get away."

"He don't ever work that hard. It's 'cause we were meeting, I'll bet, that he stayed away."

"You don't know that for sure," I said.

"Yes, I do. Yes, I do. I know that cheap tripper."

"Go on, Rico. Tell me what else about the Prophet. Wendell, right?"

"Well, he was Wendell in the beginning but soon he came to be the Prophet."

"The Prophet. All right."

"Yeah, well, that was the drug routine. I didn't know it then but he was doing the same routine with all sorts of other guys. I found out later. First, you'd get to know him. Then he'd start with his religion jive. God lives in you and wants to show you his face. You love everybody and be good and then you'll see the face of God. That's just about what he said."

"And most of it frightened you?"

"Yessir. It did. It frightened me but good. It was like he was having this spell over us." I recalled a time when as a child I had felt a similar thing. I was about Rico's age when I too had been caught in the spell of a boy in the senior class of the high school. He used to give the boys my age lectures on how to behave, and we were all taken in. He was like a generous older brother, sacrificing himself, giving freely of his own time just to be protective of us. And helpful, too, in the ways of young men. I remember thinking at the time that though he clearly was the most wonderful guy in the entire school, it nonetheless seemed strange that he never had anything better to do after school with his own friends. But I would put that thought out of my mind almost as quickly as it entered. It was none of my business. And, anyway, he cared for that small group of us and was teaching us things we needed to know and probably could not have learned from anyone else in the world.

"What else, Rico?"

"Well, let's see. I told you the sermon part and the drug part. Now comes the next part." He paused a moment, collecting his thoughts.

"This is going to seem real strange, I think," he said. "You ain't supposed to go thinking I'm a queer, though."

"Not you, man," I tried to assure him. "I've seen you in action."

"Well, let's say you've seen me giving my all. You've never seen me getting very much." He smiled sheepishly.

"Well, I know pretty much about silent guys like you. You know what they always say. The guy that does all the talking is the guy who's not really doing that much. But the guy that keeps his mouth shut, that's the guy to look out for. Anyway, something I'm learning even now is that the guys who talk a lot about girls don't really honor the girls. You know what I mean?"

"Yeah, well, not really."

"Well, if you do something with a girl, it's nobody's business."

"Right."

"Right. You keep it all private and then nobody has their reputation hurt."

"Yeah. That's right. Hey, that's good. I'm going to remember that. That's all right, man. Thanks."

I smiled at him. I doubt very seriously that I would have been able, at fifteen, to speak about sexual experiences, particularly with all the fright flying about as there now was in this room. Particularly, too, when the situation in which I was presently engaged was so reminiscent of the situation in my youth that caused all the fright in the first place. Young man with older man, religious talk, the distinctions between the sacred and the profane, or the good life and the bad life, or the God in your body, and the devil in your body making you feel uncomfortable with yourself and utterly confused.

"Well," Rico started, "one night the Prophet told us to meet him at a certain place. In the project somewhere. We were meeting kind of regular like then, maybe once, twice a week."

"That much?"

"Oh yeah. We were really going at it. Following him around after school. Seeing what he'd be doing. And the guys we used to be with, see, they treated us like something special, don't you see, because we knew the Prophet. We'd make up all these things that went on between him and us, which was all stupid, 'cause all we really had to tell them was what was really going on. That would have made it for us. But we always believed that was all strictly private. So we lied and junk like that.

"O.K. So this one night we meet at the project. Then all of a sudden I remember I've been to this apartment before. It's where I delivered that message for the Prophet that night to his girl. Estelle. Her name was Estelle. Anyway, we go up to this Estelle's place thinking we'd see her family. I even asked her where her mother was, and she grinned at me and said she was down at a welfare rally or demonstration. Something like that. So I asked where her sisters or brothers were. She just laughed and kind of slapped my cheek, you know." Rico patted his cheek. It made a funny, hollow sound. He did it again and threw me a quizzical look as though he'd just discovered a musical instrument. "Well, after a time, the four or five of us regular guys are there, just sitting around waiting for something to happen. It was a real hot night, and Estelle, she'd left some lemonade with glasses for us on the table, but when we wanted to drink it she said we had to wait. Then she turned off the lights. We could see in the room, though. Man, I'm telling you I'm getting scared just telling you about this. Then, Estelle comes back into the room and she's got her bathrobe on. We can just about see her. We're sitting there, boy, looking at her, trying to see through her clothes, you know. Then she says in this weird kind of voice, 'My friends, here is the Prophet.' Then in comes Wendell, I mean, you know, the Prophet. And he's wearing his basketball clothes and no shoes or socks. I never saw him without shoes or socks. I remember I spent a lot of time looking at his feet. They were real wide, I think. You know, long and wide, both. Anyway, the Prophet starts his talk like he always did, about God and the importance of us believing only in him."

"In God?"

"No man, in him. The Prophet."

"I see."

"So we listen like always, and he reminds us of what, you know, like we've been through together with him and everything. And all the time Estelle, she's standing off in the corner and I'm scared, man, like I've never been scared. Shit, Spider and the Taylor didn't come today so's I would have to tell you all this."

"You don't have to, Rico. It can wait. There's nothing that says you've got to speak any more about what went on with the Prophet and all."

"Oh yes there is," Rico replied. "There's plenty. Like, this is kind of a confession for me, or whatever you would call it. I feel like if I tell you I'll get all the rest of the Prophet out of me. It's like I'm going to be bleeding this story out of me. You know what I mean?"

"Yes. Like purification."

"Yes. Like . . . whatever that was you said."

"Purification?"

"Yeah. Purification, whatever that is."

"Oh, it means kind of cleansing yourself. Letting all the junk come out."

"That's what I'm doing, too, man. Letting the junk come out. But if Spider and the Taylor don't get here they'll still have all the junk trash inside of them, won't they?"

"Well, in a sense they will."

"That's right. They'll still have the junk. Man, when I think how we were so taken in by that . . . Jeez, I was just about to call him a swear and something stopped me. I tell you, man, that spell he cast is still with me. I was just going to call him by a bad name and I couldn't do it. I couldn't do it. Hey, you been slipping drugs in me when I wasn't looking?" Rico stared at me.

" 'Course not."

"You sure?"

"Of course I'm sure. Have I ever given drugs to anyone you ever heard of?"

"Well . . ."

"Huh?"

"Well, I don't . . ."

"Rico, be serious. This is important. You must know that I don't give drugs to kids, or tell them how to lead their lives. *I'm* not the Prophet, you know. I'm not the guy in the story you're telling me about." I was insistent.

"Yeah, I know all that."

He received my words as if they were a punishment. "O.K. That's good," I said. "You know what we do together is not at all what you did with this guy Wendell from the high school, four, five years ago."

"Not Wendell," he interrupted. "The Prophet."

"The Prophet. Jesus. O.K. The Prophet. But he's him and I'm me. Tom. Right?"

"Right. I know." Rico's voice was quiet. He looked as though he might have wanted to cry. I was impressed by the courage he revealed, for the fright of the earlier days remained. But I was conscious, too, of my own strong desire to make certain he not only would differentiate between me and the Prophet, but would firmly enunciate that differentiation: Say it loud, before God, is what I wanted to say to him. Now, here, before God!

"Let me tell you the rest then." Rico moved in the large overstuffed armchair. His legs were uncrossed and his feet placed flat on the floor. His left hand held his right hand in his lap. It was an unusual position for this young athlete whose normal posture was legs spread wide, and one thrown over the arm of the old chair. "So the Prophet he goes on about the pure life and what we have to know. And then he says, 'Tonight we're going to talk about women.' He says to us, 'You all know about making babies, don't you?' And we all sort of say yes and laugh, although I didn't really know everything then. Shit, this must sound weird, man. Huh?"

"No, it doesn't at all."

"Well, he tells us about making love and how good it feels when you do it. He says we should be doing it because that's the nice part of God in our bodies. Then there's all this shit about how the body is supposed to be used for some things and the mind is supposed to be used for other things. I didn't really follow everything he says. But I was sitting there. Probably with my mouth wide open. So then he says he's going to give us a demonstration and we should watch closely. I don't know then if someone put the lights on or something, but I remember that at about that point I could see everything, and I just knew that Estelle didn't have no clothes on under that robe of hers. So then he says to Estelle, 'O.K., baby, do it.' And real slowly she starts to take her robe off. Then she's all naked. Then she walks right up to each of us and lets us look at her. I remember old Taylor, he put his hand on her stomach, and she pushed it away. We were laughing then, but the Prophet told us to be quiet. And when he spoke like that you can bet we obeyed."

"Were you frightened even more now?" I asked.

"You better believe it, man. I'd seen my sisters naked a couple of times, but when they caught me looking they'd hide or run away. This girl, she was sticking everything she had right at us. I mean she was a whole lot closer to me than you are now, man. A whole lot closer." For a few seconds neither of us spoke. My thoughts had turned to the fact that many young boys had told me similar stories. Not everyone, of course, but enough to make me think that the ritual was widespread, if not common. I had experienced nothing like it as a kid. The combination of the leadership role, the training for the future, the religiosity seemed strange to me. I began to feel some of this lovely fifteen-year-old boy's fright. I felt something in my own body, something distinctly apart from the erotic sensations that his story had called forth. I have often wondered about the relationship between religious figures and sexuality. There is nothing profound about these ruminations, of course, but as a child I imagined that certain officers of the church were not men. Maybe it was the skirts or the stories I heard about piety and chastity and all the rest. Whatever it was, they were special men, to be certain, but not men. Not women either, come to think of it, but also not men. And that idea both amused and terrified me.

"We didn't touch her. The Prophet says, 'Don't touch the woman,' so we didn't. Oh, I remember, she had oil all over her body, so she was kind of shining. Jesus. Weird, huh?"

"Go on, Rico."

"Well, when she moves away, the Prophet says that we should all drink some lemonade. We did. Man, I remember I was plenty thirsty, too. Then he says, 'Now that was the woman's body and here is the man's body.' Then he takes off his basketball shirt and pants and he ain't got nothing on underneath. And he's kind of oily too. Estelle starts to touch him, but he says like, 'Cool it, Estelle, just hold on now, baby. Now what we're going to do,' he said, 'is demonstrate to you all about lovemaking.' I can't remember everything, but you kind of know what happened. Right?"

"Right."

"They were on the floor and I was sitting there wondering whether anyone was going to come home and find us. I was also thinking that if my mother knew what I was doing she'd have beat me with a belt."

"She do that?"

"She *do* that? You better believe she did. Ever since my father died . . . or went away, she took over beating us where he left off. Prophet, though, never did that. He talked hard to us once in a while. We deserved it, I suppose. But he never hit us. Never laid a hand on us. Not like my mother or father. Man, she used a belt, and when we really do something bad, she makes sure our ass feels the buckle. Big silver buckle that belonged to my old man. You get hit by that you don't forget it that easily. Don't think no one would ever forget being hit by a belt." Rico stopped, his thoughts on something more painful than the history he was recounting.

"Well, we watched them go at it. I'd never seen it like that, up close you know, but I knew what you were supposed to do. It was different with him, though, 'cause of the way we felt about him. He could've done anything and it would have been fine with us, you know. He was kind of perfect, and I never used to let on that I had any doubts. I never even mentioned to Spider or anyone that I was scared. Only that night, boy, we were all scared. We said so later." Then he hesitated for a moment. "Let's see, do you want to hear more?"

"If you got more, sure."

"I can't remember too much more about that night. Spider, he'll tell you more. He remembers all kinds of things better than I do. That's true, you know. He really does."

"I didn't know," I said, giving Rico some breathing room. At this point I was almost wishing that Spider would not arrive. Later I would ask him about his feelings and recollections, but, for now, I knew if the boys got together they would find a way to sidetrack the conversation. Each of us has different aspects that are brought forth by the people we are with, and Rico, though he would be more open with his comrades, would also tell me things and allow certain feelings to show through in my presence that might stay permanently invisible in the presence of the others.

"They were bumping around on the floor, man. I could smell the oil in the room, I remember. They knocked over this coffee table at one point and the Prophet told us to leave it where it was and concentrate just on him. Estelle made all sorts of noises. That part kind of scared me." Rico tried to imitate the groaning sounds. "I couldn't tell if she was hurting or loving it. I s'pose she must have loved it. But it was hard to see why. Pretty soon Prophet says he's done and asks who's going to be next. 'Let's have a volunteer,' he says. I don't even remember what Estelle was doing then. Just lying there I guess. 'C'mon,' he says. 'Which one's going to be a man first? This is the evening when boys get to be men. Almost.' That's what he says. 'Almost.'" Rico closed his eyes, a frown showing on his face. Again he shook his head and wiped away some perspiration on his upper lip. He looked at his finger which gleamed silver with liquid. "Man, I could practically get myself frightened all over again. Hey, man, can I tell you something funny?"

"Please."

"You're going to laugh your ass off when I tell you this."

"I doubt it." Somehow I knew that he was about to confess some naiveté about sexuality. I remembered my own deficiencies and lack of knowledge, and the fact that those men who taught me about sexuality, even in the dirty jokes and lascivious accounts I would overhear in locker rooms and gymnasiums and on beaches when the "big kids" were around, did indeed seem like prophets to me. They seemed to make my biological growth jump visible notches and then knit this growth to sociological and psychological realities. The jokes and the stories about what happened with Amy on Friday night or with Gloria in the dunes right in the middle of the morning made the perfect context for comprehending these mysterious and quasi-religious rituals. Those boys, the older boys, were prophets, all right. They were sent from heaven to destroy the angelic in us, and establish the boundaries of the sacred and the profane once and for all. They were not only capable of foreseeing the future, they *were* the future, brought to us by some astrological coincidence. We worshipped them, and followed them on the beach until our legs ached, until our skin was burned, and we longed for water. We followed them nearly into their homes, or the homes of their girl-friends, until they simply had to pay us some attention, however small — until finally they *had* to recognize us.

"No, Rico," I said, "I won't laugh. I've been there."

"Yeah, but not like this," he responded.

"Well, maybe not. I don't know yet, but I do know that shame or whatever it is you were feeling was around when I was young."

"Yeah, but I cried." He blurted out the words, his dark eyes suddenly becoming moist. "He chose me 'cause I was nearest to him, and she took my pants off and he lifted me on her and all I did was cry. And they laughed. Every one of them laughed."

"The Prophet too?"

"Yeah, the Prophet too. They all laughed. Motherfuckers. All of 'em. All of 'em full of shit up to their brown eyes." His eyes were suddenly dry and bright. Anger had kept away the tears. "They could laugh 'cause they didn't have to do nothing, but I had to lay on top of her oily old skin and smell her perfumes or whatever. . . . Shit, she smelled so bad ain't no one would've wanted to get close to her."

"Did the Prophet keep insisting that you keep trying?" It was strange, the feelings I had about this man I never knew. I despised him for the unforgivable deeds he made these boys honor and attempt. I despised him for exploiting them, their age, their level of psychological development, and for taking advantage of a situation he damn well comprehended and nourished. Yet, at the same time, I couldn't get myself to label him sick or deranged. I was trapped in the same flow Rico earlier had expressed when confessing his inability to use a swear word in conjunction with the Prophet. A strand of sacredness remained in Rico's telling as well as in my hearing.

"He did for a while," Rico recalled. "Then he said, 'Can't you do something, 'Stelle?' She tried to touch me and everything, but I was screaming and everything so they stopped. Maybe I scared them. I don't know. I wasn't about to know what they were thinking then. I just remember running out of there with my clothes and putting on my pants as fast as I could out in the stairwell, you know, and heading off, lickety-split to home. Must have set me some kind of record or something. I guess not too much else happened that night. The Taylor said they went home right after I did. Maybe one of 'em stayed on. I don't know. I didn't want to hear more about that night."

"Did you see the Prophet again after that?" I asked.

"You kiddin' me, man? 'Course I did. Saw him the next night. Had to. That was all part of the plan. I hoped he wouldn't bring Estelle with him though, but he did. I was afraid to look at them. But he didn't say anything about that night."

"Did you tell anybody else?"

"No sir. Not a living soul. I just stayed in my bed thinking."

"Thinking what, do you remember?" I smiled at him.

"Yeah. Like whether I wanted to be a man like the Prophet. Or maybe I thought I was a queer. I was really mad at Estelle, too, 'cause she'd acted like she was some hot shit broad, and who is she, anyway? Just 'cause you hang around with some big guy don't make you something so special, you know."

"I know. I've learned that."

"Yeah, well, she acted like she was some important lady who we all had to respect and dig. I liked her at first, but later she was just another asshole. They got lots of chicks like her. All she liked was screwing. Hadn't been the Prophet, would have been some other guy on the basketball team. I'll bet you that all you like."

"You're probably right."

"You know I'm right. I know her kind. I might not have known too much when I was only ten or eleven but I know her type now. Go to school right now with a whole pack of 'em just like her. When you grow up you learn about her kind. I pity the poor dumb ape going to end up with her as a wife."

Often, as I had chased after the older boys, my own prophets, I had resented the girls who had attained such a special status with them. I didn't think much about what they would do together, even when I saw them, in the summer, say, at dusk, holding hands or walking with their arms around one another, or when the boy's arm was thrown loosely over the girl's shoulder so that his hand dangled precariously close to her breast. What I imagined, quite honestly, is that they did many of the same things with the girls as they did with us, and that the girls held them in the same high esteem — I almost wrote *high priest* — as we did. The girls must follow them around, too, I thought.

But whatever went on, the boy seemed to have the ultimate power and the force of religion behind him. Surely, there was not anywhere a girl with so much power that one could feel the force and the heat of it as one did with an older boy. And something else. The boy had no private world, no inner reflections, as I, a ten-year-old, had. Everything that came to him was caught up in his charm and guile and way, so that wondering and guilt and shame and fear and doubt were not known to him. Maybe girls felt these emotions, but the older boy never did. Always he would succeed at whatever he tried, and always his actions in pursuit of his chosen destiny were undertaken with unequivocal might and balance. His strength and unyielding sense of the right and the just would prevail.

"Guy going to marry her," Rico was continuing, "going to blow his brains out pretty soon. Can't make no life with a bitch like that."

"Well, you saw the Prophet more after that though, huh?"

"Oh, yeah. I did. We all did. Shit, man, where the hell is Spider or the Taylor? I knew they wouldn't show."

"What happened then, Rico?"

"Not much, really. There was another sex thing but I didn't go. Most of the others didn't either. The Prophet, he was getting kind of strange. High on smack most of the time. Estelle too, I guess. We watched them do that too, one night, at the Prophet's house. Man, that was something, just being inside his house. It wasn't really much. Messy and all, but we was as excited about that as anything, I guess. It was like, you know, maybe going inside a church or something. I don't know what I was expecting to see. Maybe idols or statues or lots of weird-sounding music or something. But it was just a regular old apartment, like ours. But it was different. We still had it for him then." Rico waited a moment as a feeling rushed through his body. "Lookie here." He pulled up his shirt sleeve and sweater. I shuddered momentarily, fearing that he was about to show me needle marks. Oh God, I pleaded. "Lookie here," Rico repeated. "I go to thinking 'bout that first time at the Prophet's pad, and I get me all these goosebumps. I tell you, man, he had a spell on us. You just don't want to believe it."

"I do, Rico. Sure I believe it. Why do you doubt me?"

"I don't know."

"You do though, don't you?"

"Yeah. I guess. A little. Do you really believe everything I say to you?"

"Yes. Just about everything. Why? Shouldn't I?"

"I don't know. I don't think I'd believe you if you told me what I just got through telling you."

"I believe you. So maybe there's a difference?"

"There must be, 'cause it's all weird."

"Is there an end to it someplace?"

"Yeah. But that's why I wish Spider or someone were here." He looked over at the door.

"Well, maybe they'll come. Why don't you start it." I hoped that I might have a few more minutes alone with this boy. Was that such a strange desire? Could the Prophet once have felt this same way, I wondered?

"I'm skipping now," Rico said. "Maybe four, five months. Taylor, he's the oldest of us, of our gang, you know. He was just eleven or eleven and a half. Anyway, the Prophet asks him to do something one night. This was near the end . . ." Rico was stopped by the sound of Spider Wormsley entering the little room in which we were speaking.

"Caught you two together," he said.

"Where you been, man?" Rico asked. He looked relieved.

"Working. Where the hell you think I been, rapping with some dude? Hi, Tom." He grinned at me and held out his hand.

"Hi yourself," I replied. We shook hands. Spider was out of breath. He had been running to catch at least some part of my conversation with his friend.

"What you tell him?"

"Guess."

"Prophet?"

"Yeah."

"Everything?"

"Just about."

"That night with Estelle and . . . ?"

"Yeah."

"Really?" Spider was surprised but visibly proud of his friend. Rico nodded yes. "Hey, not bad. You got real guts, R.B."

"Some guts," Rico muttered.

"Yeah. You do. For a stoolie." He grinned.

"Who's a stoolie? We said we was going to tell."

"I never said nothing," Spider teased him. Rico caught on.

"Motherfucker. Working, my ass," Rico shouted at him.

"You tell him you cried?" Spider asked coarsely.

"Yeah. And that *you* ran like hell from 'Stelle too."

"Bullshit I ran. You ran, man, but I stayed right to the end."

"Yeah, so then what happened?"

"Ah, I don't remember." Spider laughed.

"You're the biggest liar I ever knew. He's the biggest liar, Tom," Rico shouted. "Don't believe him. Don't believe nothing he tells you." Rico went to playfully grab his friend. Spider pushed his arm away.

"I never lied once about the Prophet." Spider was suddenly serious. His tone was contagious and the smiles left my face and Rico's too. "I never lied, man, when it came to *that* guy. He might have been queer, man . . . Rico tell you that, Tom?"

"Yeah, kind of."

"Well, he sure was weird. He had a spell, you know?"

"Yes," I answered. "I know all about that."

"It's true. That part of it's all true. How much you tell him, R.B.?"

"To the night with the cops."

"The arrangement, you mean?"

"Yeah."

"He know about that?"

"No. You tell him."

"O.K. Ah, see, we went to his house, the Prophet's I mean, one night. R.B., the Taylor, Philly, the regular bunch. Philly's not around here anymore. So we went up to his house and we're eating sandwiches and drinking Coke and stuff like that, and the Prophet comes on with this plan of his. He thinks it's important for us to be men. You tell him all about that shit, about being mature and honest?" He looked at Rico.

"Yeah. He knows," Rico replied. He was listening as attentively as I.

"Well, he said that a real man can kill so we should help him get this cop. See there'd been . . ."

"You mean kill a policeman?" I asked.

"Yeah. That sound so strange to you, man?"

"A little."

"Shouldn't. Guess you don't spend that much time in this neck of the woods." Spider was all business; Rico seemed frightened that there should be tension between Spider and me.

"I know about plans to kill people, Spider. I didn't know that it was usual that kids of ten were in on them."

"Well, they ain't always, but sometimes they are. Like we were."

"Yeah, I guess you were."

"You want to hear this or not?" Spider asked.

"Yeah. I do."

"O.K. So he sets up a plan that we're supposed to get this cop's attention, or something, and when he comes after us the Prophet's going to whisk him out."

"Whisk him out?"

"Kill him, man. Waste him."

"Oh yeah. I see. And what were you guys supposed to do?"

"Rob a liquor store."

"Oh Jesus."

"Jesus nothing," Spider responded. "He had so many plans for us. This was just the beginning."

Rico interrupted him. "The Prophet said all the time that a man had to learn all there was to life and all there was to death, too. And the way you learned about death was by killing. So that's why he had us do it."

"I see."

"Ain't that right, Spider?"

"Yeah. That's what he said. I remember. He said life and death live in the body together. We got parts of us pushing us in the direction of life, and parts pushing us in the direction of death, and so we had to learn 'bout both."

Rico nodded as though he remembered that one sermon verbatim. "That was his philosophy," he added.

"His philosophy," I mumbled.

"Yeah. That was it. Don't you believe us?"

"Sure I do. Sure. So, did you rob the store?"

"I wanted to," Spider started, "but the other guys all chickened out."

"That's not true," Rico came back.

"Is too. You guys were all too scared. I was the only one going to do it."

"I would have too," Rico tried again.

"Well, then maybe it was the Taylor or Philly, but they outvoted me. I remember that much."

"You voted?" I was surprised.

"Yeah," Spider answered. Rico was looking at his hands and nodding. "We voted to see who would go with the Prophet."

"And?"

"Well, everyone but me . . ."

"And me," Rico got the words in.

". . . and him said no. So we didn't do it." His words were so matter-of-fact.

"Well, good old democracy." I was a bit dumbfounded. "I think that's a damn nice ending."

"Except it's not the ending," Spider responded. "'Cause the Prophet was really mad when we said no. He got us up to Estelle's one night and beat the shit out of us. Man, you remember that, don't you?" Rico remembered. "Boy, did he ever whup us good. Hit us with this rope of his. It really hurt. He told us he was cleansing us or something, and that we were all evil."

"I guess we really must have been," Rico muttered without looking up. "He sure wanted that cop dead."

"Was it a white cop?" My question slipped out. I didn't think I meant to ask it.

"No, man. He was no white man. He was black like me. Blacker even. Like the Taylor."

I tried to laugh off what I thought would be the end of their story. "Yeah?"

"Well, they planned another thing with us robbing and him getting the cop."

"Who's they?"

"Estelle and the Prophet. The two of 'em together."

"I see."

"So the particular night comes, and we break into the store like we was told and just make a lot of fuss and everything." Spider's account reeked with confidence. Rico, however, appeared frightened. He kept looking back and forth between his friend and me. "Then the sirens are going on and all hell's breaking loose. I even think the fire department was in on it. There was a fire in the next block or something, and they were already in the neighborhood. Something like that."

All Rico could utter was, "Yeah."

"So they caught you?"

"Oh sure. All of us. We hadn't gotten five steps. I remember all I had was a bottle of some mix that was sitting on the counter. Rico here, he didn't have anything."

"What about the metal window covers?" I asked naively.

"The Prophet cut the lock on it somehow. On the door, too, you know?"

"So did the policemen come?"

"By the millions, man. You should've seen 'em. It was unbelievable." Spider now did all the talking. Rico just looked at me. "They were swarming around like flies on a pile of shit, man. Everywhere, man. I mean everywhere."

"And the Prophet got his man?"

"He got him all right. Flung his knife into the guy's back."

"Jesus," I muttered. Rico looked sick. Spider spoke quickly.

"I didn't see that, man. I mean, I'm just telling you what I heard."

"He die?" I asked.

"No. They took him to the hospital and they saved his life. The doctors and everyone there. They saved his life."

"They fixed his lung," Rico said.

"I see. I see. This has been one afternoon, hasn't it?" I muttered. Rico smiled at me.

"You better believe it." He was utterly exhausted and relieved and ready to go. Rarely have I sat this long with a boy his age. But Spider, I could see, had more to tell.

"What is it, Spider?"

"Well, you got to hear the end."

"You're right. Go on."

"See, they took the Prophet away. They got him locked up now somewhere, man. We don't even know where. They say in Roslindale, but we don't know for sure."

"But why," I interrupted, "was he so damned intent on getting this one cop?" As I asked the question, my mind, for some reason, spelled out the letters of my own words. I imagined that I had capitalized the H in *he*.

"Because the cop had raped Estelle two different times and the police said they didn't know who it was, and twice he got her and everyone knew who did it. So the Prophet took revenge. Just like he taught us. Right?" Spider's words were drenched with pride and manly confidence. Rico was nodding his head faster and faster. "He always told us you got to fight for your honor, and that's what he did, man. He did the

56   *The Voices of School*

right thing, man. Anybody can see that. He was a good man. Ain't nobody going to disagree with that."

"Nobody," echoed Rico.

"You'd do the same thing for your old lady, Tom. Wouldn't you do it if what happened to Estelle happened to her?"

"You would, wouldn't you, man?" Rico was staring at me, his mouth open.

"I'd sure feel like doing it," I stammered, "but I don't know that I would actually get around to doing it. I mean, that's really . . ."

"Well, then you maybe ain't the man the Prophet was," Spider concluded. Rico was not as convinced. I looked at him, a boy half my age, for help. "No sir, you ain't half the man the Prophet was," Spider repeated.

"You believe that, Spider?" I questioned him.

"Right on. That's what life's all about. That's what living in the streets is all about. You ain't got no friends going to help you out. A guy messes around with your old lady, you got to go slash him up." He chopped at the air. "Slash him up right, for good."

"I get what you mean, but I wonder . . ."

"There ain't no wondering. That's what the Prophet did. He made his decision and that's what he did. I tell you, he's a good man. You trust a man like that. I ain't got many heroes but he's sure one." Spider's voice had momentarily become hoarse.

"Is he one of your heroes too, Rico?" I asked. Rico looked away from me, while Spider started to answer for his friend.

"Damn right he is. Ain't he, Rico?"

"Let Rico answer." My tone was suddenly harsh.

"Go ahead, Rico," Spider said.

"I ain't got many heroes either," Rico began. "But the Prophet, he's still one of my heroes. He meant more to me than anyone alive. He was the man. Only man I ever knew. You believe in somebody like that, you got to go along with everything he says and does. I was scared a lot, like I told you, when I was a kid, but there wasn't nobody else in the whole world took the time to bother with me like he did. So, yeah. He's still the Prophet for me."

"Me too," came from Spider. We stood up, none of us speaking.

"I'm going to have to meet the Prophet," I said finally.

"Hey, that would be great. Can you find him? Crazy." They were both yelling and filled with excitement. It was almost the same excitement one encounters among ten- and eleven-year-olds.

"You think you can find him?" Spider asked.

"Maybe he's dead," Rico reflected aloud.

"I'll try. I'll do my best. I'll get his full name, his old address, and stuff like that. He may be dead, like you say, though I don't know why he should be."

"Hey, that's good, man."

"You're all right, man."

"What a man, eh Spider?"

"Yeah, he's all right."

"I always knew you were all right, daddy."

We were just about out the door and into the snowy day when I asked: "Hey, you guys, if I do find him, would you want to see him?" The question silenced them. Their postures slumped, revealing a diffidence if not worry.

"Well, ah, I don't think so, man," Spider responded. "I mean, I'd like to know how he is and all that, but I'd just as soon let you see him."

"Yeah. You see him, Tom, and report to us like we always got to report what we do to you. You see him without us, O.K.?"

"O.K. That's fine with me. Is there some fright still, though, in seeing him?" They hunched up their shoulders trying as best as they could to deny it. "Maybe a little," I said, not even as a question. They nodded yes, and turned their eyes away from me. "The spell still holds, doesn't it?" Again they nodded yes; then they turned to leave. Spider went out first; Rico held the door open for me.

"Watch you don't slip out here," Spider called to me from the icy street. "Don't want nothing happening to you."

chapter three

the
ghetto
scientists

culture as teacher

for several years I have been meeting with groups of young boys and girls from the South End area of Boston. They come from several schools and there is no telling who might show up on a particular Tuesday afternoon. Our after-school conversations, which if the weather permits we hold outside on the grass of a nearby play area, range across any and all topics.

One afternoon, for example, we got to speaking about science and what they believed scientists do. Strangely, as important as science is in our culture, it is often omitted in discussions of grammar school and high school education. But what these young children from a poverty area in Boston show us is how culture, social class, and community influence people's personal development as well as the content of their impressions and knowledge. The reader will see that the discussion in chapter three varies from accurate, even astute impressions of science, to impressions that appear to be embroidered with fantasy and make-believe. We could easily grade these young people according to whether their responses are right or wrong. But if we did, we would be guilty of listening only for facts about science and overlooking something far more important: namely, what their knowledge tells us about them and the portion of the culture in which they are growing up.

A word of caution: The visions and impressions of these children, influenced as they are in part by personal predispositions and by cultural and social factors, reveal an enormous variety and richness. It is improper, therefore, to think of these imaginative, searching children as being wrong in their answers, or, even worse, disadvantaged. They have learned well about science, and one hopes that school and future experiences will provide them additional information but not disparage either the information they now possess or the present sources of this information.

It is difficult to say how many of us were speaking that afternoon in the little park near the hospital. So much was going on — a colossal basketball game, boys darting after girls, a pretend fight — that our population kept shifting. Still, there were always four or five young people, about ten years old, who joined me on the grass alongside the basketball court, and the conversation tumbled along so that we all could follow it and the newcomers could be cued in easily. The boys and girls were speaking about school, their studies, teachers, parents, and brothers and sisters, although there was an unusual side trip into politics. In times like these I wish I could be totally free to say anything to young people. It is not so much that I am thinking anything particular about them, as that I am holding back ideas that for one reason or another I feel should remain hidden. Maybe it has to do with the laziness of the day or the fact that none of the young people seems especially eager to latch onto some topic. Maybe it is the way some of us do research: entering poor areas of cities and speaking with people, letting conversations run on without interpretation or analysis. Maybe, too, some of us have a strong desire to know what these people think of us and the work we do.

I think that desire is what got us going one afternoon last year toward the end of spring. My job at M.I.T., the term *social scientist*, and a series of other references gradually launched a discussion about who scientists are and what they do. It was, in fact, the only topic of the afternoon that held the young people's attention, and though at first my sometimes uncontrollable clinical intuitions suggested that a discussion about scientists was for them a comfortable means of revealing their feelings about me and my work with them, this was not the case. All of them, obviously, had thought about scientists and the work of science. Moreover, in their expressions, I heard their feelings about various parts of their culture and their country. Truthfully, the idea of going to a group of boys and girls whose mothers are on welfare, and whose homes show such blight it would sicken the most stoic and reserved among us, and asking them to speak about their perceptions of scientists seems absurd to me, if not utterly exploitative. And yet, here we were in Boston's South End, sitting on the grass, hearing the basketball pounding on the cement, and the sounds of cars and children and dogs, and speaking, of all things, about scientists.

"Now I'm going to tell you what they do." Ten-year-old McNeil Henderson stood up. "First of all they wear white coats," he said. "They got to do that to keep the germs away from 'em."

"What you talkin' about, germs?" Ronald Fletcher asked angrily. "Sit down, Mack. You don't know what you're talkin' about."

"Hell I don't," Mack answered. "Scientists work with germs. Got things so small you can't even see 'em. That's the thing about scientists. They're working all the time with things you can't even see. . . ."

"Then how they work with 'em?" Carol Lamont wondered, looking at me for support. I nodded at her as if to say I thought it a perfectly reasonable question.

"They got microscopes. They can see things nobody else can see."

"Yeah? Is that a fact?" Carol asked.

"That's a fact, man! Tell 'em, Tom."

"They got microscopes, all right . . ." I said.

"They work under the ground in places where no one can find 'em either." Gerald Truman, who was called "Carolina," picked up on the conversation. "Scientists hide out under the ground. Got all these laboratories and equipment and stuff. Got it all stored under the ground. Could be anywhere. Nobody knows where they work 'cause if they did all their secrets would be let out. Could be working under us right now. Right where you're sitting, Fletch."

"You got to be out of your mind. Ain't no one working under there but the sewer people," Fletch retorted. "Here, I'll dig it up and show you." He grabbed at some grass and began pulling it up. The others laughed, although some looked to see what Fletch might have uncovered in the hole.

"'Lina, you don't know what you're saying. Scientists work in the universities and colleges. They don't work underground *or* above ground. They work like everybody else. You can go see 'em." One could perceive that Mack did not like Jackie Snowden's assuredness. He was already preparing to debate her.

"You don't know nothing either, Jacqueline," he began. "Girls don't know about science."

"Yes we do. We've got science in our school."

Mack was chagrined. "That ain't science! That ain't nothing. No science going on in school. Maybe they got teachers teaching about science, like, you know, nature, but that ain't science. No one even knows what scientists are 'til something really big happens. Like the spaceships, things like that. That's when they're really making science, or like when they find all kinds of things in the ocean, that'll be science too, someday. But none of that's happening in school. We just read books in school. That ain't what anybody means by science."

"He's right, man." It was a boy named Cleo whom I didn't know. "The thing about scientists not seeing anybody is because they don't speak no language anybody knows 'til they get to be scientists. Part of being a scientist, see, is just getting to know those languages. That's what they got to study for."

"You mean that scientists don't speak like you and me? I mean, English? They don't speak English?" Incredulous, Carol's eyes opened wide.

"That's right. You don't know nobody ever talked with a scientist. Never seen one, neither."

"Yeah? How about on the television when they go to the moon and they talk with all those guys?" Jackie protested.

"Them guys is astronauts."

"No, the other guys." Fletch picked up the question.

"No sir. No scientists. Got all these guys that run them dials and make all them things, but those aren't scientists. No, no. Scientists ain't involved with that."

"Well, so what they do then, if they ain't working on spaceships?" Jackie asked.

"I'll tell you." Mack cut her off. "They're hidden away working on problems you and I could never once dream about. Fact is, when we dream about 'em it's only because the scientists have already made us dream about 'em."

"I don't understand what any of you are talking about." Jackie was shaking her head. "I think you're all crazy, is what I think." They laughed. Mack and Cleo momentarily fought for the right to speak.

"Let me tell 'em. Let me tell 'em."

"C'mon, Cleo. Let Mack talk."

"I'll tell 'em. I'll tell 'em." Excited, Mack had remained standing. Even when someone else spoke and he had nothing to say he tried to interrupt. "Here's, here's what it is. Now you look around and you'll see the trees and the ground and the sky. Right?" They all answered, right. "Okay now. What scientists do is make these things the way they are."

"Aw, cut it out."

"You crazy, man? That's nature. That ain't science." Everyone seemed to believe Mack to be heretical.

"Naw, that's true," he argued. "You want to know what scientists do?"

"Yeah. But *you* can't tell us."

"He don't know what he's talking 'bout, Carolina."

"Scientists right now, somewhere, are working to make the sky change color. They're going to make it blue, then they're going to make it green or gold or red." Suddenly everyone was quiet. We all looked at Mack. Even Fletch was impressed. "They're going to change the sun too. Going to make it hot and cold, and the clouds too."

"What they going to do with the clouds?"

"Well, I don't know for sure. But they'll do something."

"Maybe make 'em go away forever." Carol was caught up in Mack's vision.

"Naw. They can't do that," Jackie said.

"Hell they can't," said Cleo. "That's the whole thing like Mack here was saying. What you and I are thinking about, that ain't anywhere near what scientists are thinking about. They're living in a world all by themselves. Ain't no one can touch 'em, ain't no one going to understand what they're saying until they want us to understand. Someday you're going to get up out of your bed and look up at the sky and it's going to be all gold or silver, then you'll know scientists been fixin' with it."

"Could be. Could be," several of them agreed. "They going to mess with water too?" Carol asked.

"Everything you put in your mouth scientists going to fix with." Cleo was taking charge. "All kinds of food. Everything going to be different."

"What do you mean, different?" Carol asked.

"They're going to change all the food . . ." Mack sought to continue but he was cut off.

"That don't make no sense. Scientists don't do anything with food. Food's food. You grow it in the ground or make it."

"Scientists eat the same food we eat." Several of the young people giggled. I heard jokes about blueberry pie, peanut butter, and hot dogs.

"Ain't no one changing peanut butter. That's from the ground. You don't *science* peanut butter."

"You could if you wanted," Cleo argued.

"Yeah, how?"

"Food isn't science."

"Scientists can do anything they want with food. They can make it real good. And they can poison you too."

"They can?" Many became serious again, although around the edges of the group a few still joked and exchanged lists of foods they especially liked or disliked. "How they going to poison us?" Jackie inquired.

"*Are* they going to poison us?"

"I tell you, you guys don't know what's going on." Fletch was adamant.

"Oh yeah? They probably got scientists right now figuring out ways to poison the enemy."

"Like who?"

"I don't know."

"Russians, maybe."

"Yeah, the Russians. They can make food look just like it was real. Tastes real and everything, but it's not real. Guy eats it and falls over dead. Like that. Wham!" The girls were shocked. For some reason Carol looked at her hands. "They can put germs in the food and kill people." Cleo had sparked Mack, and while Fletch tried to convince the others that neither boy knew anything about science, the rest of the group was transfixed.

"Food and water is what scientists are messing with all the time. All they got to do is put some of their stuff in the water and they can kill anybody. Gets in your throat and gags you." Mack pretended to choke himself. Profanity emanated from the basketball court. "Choke and gag you and then everyone's dead. Everyone everywhere going to be dead if the scientists want."

"You mean it's like magic?" Carolina asked.

"Aw, cut that crap," Fletch insisted. Cleo and Mack were undaunted.

"Yeah, it's kind of like magic," Cleo admitted.

"Like religion too," Mack echoed.

"How's that?" I asked, even more intrigued than before.

" 'Cause the only people really messing with life and death are scientists and people in the church. Living and dying are what all those people do. They got all kinds of secret information that nobody else has." His explanation appeared to convince most of the others.

"Only soldiers kill," Fletch suggested.

"And cops," several of the others added almost in unison. "And cops, yeah."

"And scientists," Cleo said quietly. "They can kill without anyone knowing. Sneaking around doing what they're doing. They can kill all right, and nobody's smart enough to figure out how they go about doing what they're doing."

"They can save lives too." Jackie seemed to have been won over to the other side.

"That's right." Cleo and Mack joined her. Carolina and the girls were listening intently, but Fletch walked away for a moment. Two more boys had joined the group, and he was filling them in, inserting his own biases and perceptions as he did.

"Like science in the school?" one of the new boys questioned him. "That kind of stuff? My brother takes chemistry in high school."

"Naw. Real chemistry, real science," Fletch advised him. The first boy seemed satisfied.

"Yeah, they can save any life they want," Mack was continuing.

"Like doctors, Mack?"

"Better."

"Right," Cleo supported his partner.

"Better even. Doctors, see, don't really figure things out. They just know what to do. You got a headache, like, they learned what pill to give you. But science invents the pills. They make 'em. Design 'em in their heads and then everybody's got 'em."

"That's right. Who do you think invents those pills? Doctors don't." The word invent was assuming special significance for the group. I overheard Jackie say to Carol:

"No one invented trees or grass."

"No, God maybe did that," Carol replied, "but scientists made the colors and the shapes. They had a reason for that stuff to be green."

"I think it's because green is easiest on your eyes," Jackie said.

"Me too. That's what I learned too." (As a child, I had heard the same explanation along with the notion that the sky reflected the color of the water on the earth's surface.) The boys had not heard any of this other conversation.

"See, what happens," Cleo was explaining to Carolina and Fletch, "is, you take something like an airplane. Scientists don't really need to bother inventing that. Regular men do that. But what flies the plane is where scientists get asked to help out."

"Maybe they're asked. Not always," Mack corrected him.

"Yeah, maybe. That's right. Maybe they don't too, 'cause they're busy working on all sorts of more complicated things."

"More complicated than sending a guy to the moon?" one of the newcomers questioned.

"Much more. That's simple. Any of those guys can do that; scientists can do that easy. That's simple to learn."

"I doubt it," the newcomer mumbled. "That's pretty hard. Ain't no one I know can do that."

"Science teachers could," someone suggested.

"Hell they could," Cleo responded. "All they know's what's in those books they have us read. Ain't nothing in those books that tells you how to get a man walking on the moon."

"And bring him back," his friend added.

"Yeah, that's even harder." They nodded their heads up and down.

"You think that's hard for a man who can speak all the languages in the world?" Mack asked, as though pulling his trump card.

"All the languages in the world?" Carol repeated, astonished, as was I.

"Scientists speak 'em all," Mack informed us. "Ain't nothing they don't know. Their minds are like those machines, you know, with all that information and stuff in 'em . . ."

"Computers," Fletch muttered, grudgingly lending aid to his friend.

"That's it, man. They got computers in their heads. They remember everything they ever had told to 'em and everything everybody else knows too." At this point Fletch looked at me as if to say, Can't *you* stop them? Moments before I had had the feeling that Cleo and Mack might have been teasing their friends, but they were perfectly serious.

"Nobody's born with that stuff in their heads!" Fletch blurted out, seeing I would not assist him.

"Hell they ain't," Mack shot back. "You ever know these kids going to be scientists? They got brains a hundred times bigger than yours. They know everything. They're *born* that way. Lot of 'em got mothers and fathers dumber than dogs. But the kids are geniuses. They know everything. All at once when they begin to talk everybody gets to realizing just how smart they really are."

"They're brilliant," Cleo said.

"I know a boy like that at Demming," Carol was saying. "He *is* brilliant. He wants to be a scientist too. Boy, you should hear him count. Faster than a machine."

"He ain't got no choice," Mack said. "He's got to be a scientist. God's telling him he's got to be a scientist. Nothing else God's going to let him do 'cause he's so smart. Too smart to be doing anything else . . ."

"There's lots of smart people aren't scientists," Fletch interrupted. "You're talking all kind of hooey."

"Hooey nothing," Cleo argued, pointing at Fletch. "You just don't know."

"I know as much as *you* do. *You* ain't no scientist!"

"I know I ain't."

"Never going to be one neither."

"I know. So?"

"So nothing. Only you're putting all these stupid ideas in our minds and we're going to have to throw 'em out soon's we leave here."

"Hey, maybe that makes Mack a scientist." It was Carolina. "He was just saying we know all kinds of things but we don't know why we're knowing 'em. So maybe he's a scientist. That's the way I figure it, anyway." Mack beamed and Cleo punched him playfully on the shoulder. Fletch glared. Because she was watching the basketball game, Jackie had missed Carolina's deduction.

"Tom," Fletch broke in, "you going to tell these guys they're out of their minds? You going to tell 'em?"

"That's some job, Fletch," I tried. "I don't want to referee this. Let's get the ideas out on the table first." Mack had not heard me. He was angry at Fletch for calling him crazy.

"Let me tell you, Fletcher, I know a lot about scientists and what they do. I got feelings about 'em. I read and watch all that stuff on television. They're born geniuses too. God has a certain number of people he wants to be scientists. They grow up geniuses not caring about money or eating or where they live and stuff like the rest of us. They get all messed up with a whole different kind of world than we do. No one sees 'em. No one gets to talk to 'em. That's why we don't know that much about 'em. They can do things to the sky and to the stars and the ground and water and everything. They can make all different kinds of parts for your body. They can play with your brain. That's something else no one knows about too."

"Oh, cut it out."

"Let him talk. What they do to your brain?" Jackie asked.

"They make it breathe," Mack answered her. "They can put stuff in it and take stuff out. That's the kind of stuff they're experimenting with. They can get us to have thoughts if they want to."

"Ain't true!"

"Is too."

"Shut up. Let him finish."

Mack had more to say. "Anything a person can do with his mind a scientist does better."

"And faster," Cleo added.

"Right. Faster. Like, some of us add good, and some of us spell good or read good, things like that. But scientists do all that better and faster than anybody."

"What do they do with all they got in their minds?" Carol wanted to know.

"Anything they want. They figure out problems that need solving and then they go and solve 'em."

"What kind of problems?" Carolina asked.

"Oh, I don't know. Stuff with all kinds of, like, lots of numbers on the blackboard and all kinds of chemicals."

"Secret stuff," Cleo chimed in.

"Yeah, secret stuff. Why we're living now."

"You guys are really crazy." Fletch began to walk away again. I asked him to stay a bit longer.

"Why are we living now?" Jackie asked Mack.

"Don't know yet. Science has to tell us. Those guys can figure out what happened a jillion million years ago. They can tell. They study rocks and the air and they can tell who was alive and where they were and what they were doin'."

"Like, they'll find out if they had anything better than we got now hundreds and millions of years ago," suggested Cleo. "And if they find something then they'll figure out ways for us to have it too. Or they'll tell whether there's anyone else alive on the earth so's we can . . ."

"Not on the earth, dummy." For the first time Mack had corrected his ally. "They see whether there are people on other earths. You know, in space. Like, on the stars or planets."

"That's right. Other places but not on earth," Cleo agreed.

"So do they know if there are other people?"

"I thought it was only Mars," a newcomer offered.

"They know. They know all right." Mack spoke with authority.

"Then what they find?" Fletch asked.

"Don't know, 'cause nobody can read what they say in their books. Only a few people in the world can understand what scientists are saying. It takes regular people years and years just to figure out what scientists know."

"You mean they got answers to things and nobody knows what their answers are?"

"That's right," Mack answered Carolina. "Ain't nobody, not even the government knows what those guys are doing or talking about because they're so smart."

"Then I don't understand what's so good about 'em," Carol said, "if they know answers and we can't figure out what they're saying. If they speak English like us then why don't they go on television and tell us all we need to know. Or write books. Like with pollution."

"Yeah, how's that?" the rest chimed in.

"Answer her," Fletch demanded, waving his hand in Jackie's direction. Mack seemed unperturbed.

"They could go on television anytime they want. They even invented other things like television they could show us. But no one would understand."

"Well, they ought to try and see."

"Science teachers could understand 'em." The newcomer was serious but the others began to laugh.

"They don't understand nothing," they yelled out between fits of laughter. "I know more than they know. All they know's about leaves and trees."

"Hey, you guys," Cleo brought the crowd up short, "you ever think who invented fire?"

"Fire?"

"Scientists *invent* fire?"

"Must have."

"Hey. Wow!"

Mack looked especially proud. Even Fletch was silent for a few moments. I was sure we were all entertaining fantasies of underground scientists fiddling with test tubes and paraphernalia of all sorts until suddenly fire was invented. The group looked convinced.

"Now *I'm* going to speak." It was Fletch. "You sit down, Mack. C'mon! I been sitting here pretty polite. But I'm speaking now. You two guys," he pointed to Mack and Cleo, "got to shut up." The crowd mumbled words about equal time and fair arguments. "Here's what *I* think. I think scientists are no different than anybody. They may be smarter, but they ain't smarter than a lot of folks. And they don't talk all kinds of languages. They're like anybody. Fact is, if they ain't wearing their white coats, then you would pass 'em on the street and not even know who they are. And they got lady scientists too. Lots of 'em, I think.

What they're doing is trying to make the world better, like with pollution and health and stuff like that. I don't think they can mess up the color of the sky, but maybe they can, but they could do a lot of other things if they wanted to."

"Like what?" the others shouted.

"Like end hunger. They could invent food for all people. Real cheap food, so's nobody would be hungry. And they could invent different kinds of money so's more people could have money. And they could fix up cities and stuff . . ."

"Scientists don't do that kind of thing," Carolina challenged him.

"Yeah, well if they're so smart, fixing up cities ought to be easy for 'em, is what I think," Fletch said. "And they could make the weather better, like have it snow less or something. But they may not be trying to do that." The others seemed confused.

"Hey, you know you sound crazy to me," Mack yelled out.

"I ain't no more crazy than you are. I just don't think scientists have to be anybody special is all. Be just like you and me. Or Tom. Tom could be a scientist if he wanted to, couldn't you, Tom?"

"Well, a social scientist, I guess."

"There. You see?" Fletch said. "He's kind of a scientist maybe, and he ain't nobody special."

"He's smarter though," Carol said.

"That's just 'cause he's older," Fletch responded. "When we're as old as him we'll be that smart too. Won't we, Tom?"

"Yes, you will," I answered.

"'Cept poor people like us don't get to be scientists." It was Carolina. His words were spoken without emotion. "Nobody I know where we live is a scientist. Nobody's even a teacher like Tom is."

"No black people, either," said Jackie.

"That right?" Carol wondered.

"I don't know anybody. Maybe they got some. You never see 'em though." All of this was said without feelings. Suddenly they were thoughtful, dispassionate scientists, stating what they believed to be facts, and suggesting how they had derived their conclusions. Then they were quiet, some of them looking down, others regarding me, others turning to watch the basketball game. I heard the elevated train pass behind the apartment buildings on Washington Street.

Within minutes the group disbanded, talking again about what had preoccupied them for the last hour and making all sorts of plans. Carol and Mack suggested a time for another meeting. They wanted to show me an empty lot they had discovered near Dudley Street. Carol told me that her mother might have to enter the hospital for an operation. She did not know any details. I told her I would call her home and she smiled.

Fletch was the last to leave. "I didn't mess up, did I?" he questioned me, playing with blades of grass.

"Not at all. I thought what you said was great."

He seemed pleased. "I don't really know anything about scientists, 'cept that I guess I can't be one."

"Yes you can," I replied forcefully. He was not listening. "Something wrong, Fletch?"

"Well, naw, well . . . You ain't mad that I don't think you're a scientist are you?"

"No," I laughed. "I don't think of myself really as a scientist."

He watched the others walking away. "Me neither. I don't think of myself as a scientist neither." He was looking down.

"Do you think of yourself as anything, Fletch?"

"Just poor, I suppose." He did not look up.

chapter four

the other world of baby eyes ellison

on self-education

Our concerns in the last two chapters have been with the education of young people in the ghetto. Education directly by one's peers and indirectly by one's culture and community was a prominent theme in these chapters. No one, however, must get the idea that ghetto children never experience so-called traditional or formal education. They do. Despite the impressions we may have of people growing up in poverty, it is essential that we acknowledge the many truths about these people and their educational histories.

Bobby Ellison is eleven years old. He lives not too far from the neighborhood of the young ghetto scientists. Twice each week he visits a branch of the Boston Public Library to check out and return the books he reads voraciously. On several occasions I have traveled to the library with him and have heard him tell of his love for books and his intense desire to be educated in what we consider the traditional ways. To be sure, this young man learns from his peers and family, and from his culture and religion. But he is also being educated by books which he cherishes and which constitute what he calls his other world.

There is more to be told about Bobby Ellison. But I wanted, somehow, to leave this one chapter unusually short, believing that its message is pure and straightforward and needs no elaboration.

Bobby Ellison, a young man of eleven from Boston's Dorchester region, got the name "Baby Eyes" from one of his older sisters. Darlene always said that he had "the prettiest big old baby eyes of anyone in the family which was a rotten shake because one of the four girls should have gotten them." Bobby himself claims his eyes have continued growing because he reads so much. "I'm not joking," he told me one afternoon in the district library. "A man told me that if you read a lot, like maybe two books every week, your brain gets bigger and then, 'cause your eyes are part of your brain, your eyes get bigger too." He did not wait for my response, for he was busy checking out several books, something he does every Tuesday and Saturday.

"What you got today?" the young librarian asked him.

"Book on ships, book on Egypt, and this one here." He showed her a child's story with a mouse and a toadstool on the cover. "That one's for my brother. He can't read yet 'cause he's too young, but I'll read it to him." She stamped the books as he waited in front of the high counter looking up at her as if she were preparing ice cream sodas. When she finished he clasped the books to his chest. "Got 'em. Let's go so's I can start my reading."

For reasons we all know, a narrowly circumscribed picture of ghetto children is regularly drawn for us. Ironically, the hurt that they experience daily in untenantable houses and inhuman schools and the illnesses and dangers that threaten their vulnerabilities often keep us from knowing them and learning what constitutes their lives. Indeed, some of us who do politics and research in their communities but still reach our own homes in time for our own dinners, forget the strength of these children and the personal and intellectual adventures they undertake. Granted, there are children whose spirits have been assaulted by poverty, by the machinations and coerciveness that frequently substitute for education, and whose bodies have been damaged by hunger, by lead, and by cars that might have stopped had the city been able to muster funds for additional traffic lights. But despite spiritual and physical damage, and despite the temptations offered by those who mill in the streets, or who sit passively before the images of television, there are children who have encountered the world of books and entered upon that life of the mind which new information and new voices of other human beings guarantee.

"They're my other world, books are," Bobby said once. "Nothing, nothing more important to me than these books. My mother always says that if I keep reading and keep learning new things, I'll have something inside me no one ever can take away. Like, I got facts in my head that I'll bet nobody knows, 'cepting those people read those books. But some books, like, I can see from the stamps in 'em, ain't no one read. I could be the first person ever read those books. Only two people then read those books. Me and the person who wrote 'em. We're the only two. And that's all right 'cause it's like he was talking to me personal. You know what it's like? You can hear the person but you don't have to use your ears. And if you really get good, you don't have to use your eyes." He saw my confusion. "Well, you know, of course you're using your eyes to read, but pretty soon, if you get all caught up with it, you aren't seeing the writing, you're seeing what the author is telling you to see. Like boats, and pyramids, and kings, and all the people in those old cities they used to have in history. That's when you're really reading. You can't even remember what page you're on or when you turned the page. You're just into it like you were a part of it. Like you get right inside the book 'stead of it sort of getting inside of you. You know what I mean?"

I nodded yes. His manner seemed so pure, and as he spoke I recalled a conversation of almost ten years ago with a well-meaning woman in Chicago. We were seeking money and books to replenish libraries for children in the South. Generous and tolerant of our complaints and proposals, she wondered whether there were in fact poor children who even knew about books, much less found time to read them.

"Know what gets me?" Bobby interrupted my thoughts, "is the way you see some people handling books. They bend the covers way back or they'll fold a page over 'cause no one ever showed 'em how you're supposed to do it." He demonstrated the proper treatment. "See? Like that. Do that and a book will last longer than you and me both. That's long too. Longer than my mother and father, and the library too." Then he paused, examining the books he held. "Tonight I'm going to Egypt. Thousands of years ago is where I'll be. No one going to find me either 'cause I'll be hiding out in my special imagination. That's what I call it. You can always make yourself think things in your mind, even without books. But when you read, it's my other world I get to see and hear, and it don't cost anyone anything. My mother says that reading's going to help to change me, make me become something, I guess, think things different from other people. She's probably right too, 'cause she knows a lot. You should see, she's always reading. She says if you just take in what you're living and keep reading, won't be anybody in the world bigger inside than you. And that's what counts."

leo's child in the age of aquarius

family, role, and the process of socialization

Marty Ballam and I met quite accidentally. In my efforts to get to know another family, I attended a Saturday morning football game in a southern Illinois town. On the sidelines I began speaking with Marty and gradually came to know her and her family.

Marty's experiences and private thoughts would be called by many typical of the normal middle-class girl growing up. Indeed, the experiences examined in chapter five could be subsumed under the heading of socialization. Discussions of social adaptation, maturity, intimacy, relationships with parents, siblings, and classmates, sexuality, education, and the meaning of school constitute major portions of this chapter. Granted, Marty Ballam's life is different from the lives of the young people described in earlier chapters, but there is a peculiar burden that she too carries. For, ironically, young people like her coming from America's middle class and manifesting no serious psychological or academic problems are often overlooked or found uninteresting. Regarding themselves as "overly normal," unexciting, or unworthy of attention, they feel the responsibility of not being allowed to falter or stray from the destiny that their families and culture seek to create. School, moreover, is meant to enhance their sense of security and make them well-behaved and competent people.

But the conversations with Marty that follow ought to make us question the utility of a notion like "the normal student" and reexamine the ethics that underlie, or ought to underlie, our inquiries and explorations of all our students.

Marty Ballam looks almost exactly like her mother. Even at fifteen, she has the same mature, wise face, the same wide-set eyes, pale white skin, and, as everyone has noticed, the same long blonde hair that on special occasions she'll pile as high as she can on her head, and then tuck under and clip with a shiny silver medallion her grandmother had made into a pin.

"She always looks so nice that way," Marjorie Ballam said. "But try to get these youngsters to wear their hair like that to school. The younger generation! You'd think we were suggesting they go in evening gowns. Everything has to be so casual, so unkempt, so cool. Isn't that what they say? Got to be cool, man. Do your own thing." She laughed. "Seriously, Marty's really a wonderful girl though. She always was. We never had any trouble with her. Never. She always did like she was told. Not one of those kids who you have to say something twenty times before they even give you a 'huh?'. Marty's a very fine young lady. We're very proud of her. Yes. Very proud of her. She's going to be all right, too. She's not going to set any school on fire or break records, you know. But she's going to be, you know, like they say, solid citizen number one, and this country could sure use some people like that. It's getting to be, you don't know what's going to happen next, or who's going to be breaking into your house when. Don't you think that's true?" And she sighed deeply.

Marty Ballam was born about two and a half miles from her house on Michigan Street, the only house in which she has ever lived.

"What's really neat about that, is that my mother was born in the same month at the same hospital. And guess what? The same doctor who delivered me delivered her. No wait. Wait. I just learned how to say that. No, you have to say, the doctor who delivered her, delivered . . . no, the doctor who delivered her mother delivered her. He was the same doctor. Oh, you know. Dr. Ryle is about eighty-five. He's still alive. We see him all the time. Mom calls him up on my birthday. Teddy had a different doctor when he was born. Dr. Ryle had retired and he got us Dr. Abelson. He's really cute. In fact, he's a doll. Some of my friends always try to figure out ways to hang around the hospital just so we can see him maybe. He's very tall and has very strange, dark eyes. He looks like an Arabian but I'm sure he's Jewish. Anyway, that's Dr. Abelson. Maybe I'll be a nurse. Not really, I'm just kidding.

"Anyway, what I wanted to tell you was that every day Mom and I get to read our horoscopes together since it's the same one for both of us. We're both Leo. I don't know so much about it. We don't really take it all that seriously but you'd be surprised. Like last week, Wednesday, it said you had better be prepared for something like bad. No, they said upsetting but not long-lasting sadness. You're not going to believe this but that very afternoon I got a D— on a French test which I took, you know, before then, and Mom got a bill so large from Sears she practically hit the ceiling. Dad had to write the accounting department because there just had to be some mistake made. So they were right. It's really eerie."

But how does one feel, I wondered, in this the age of the "impulsive now," as "the kids" squirm in their places, fight the establishment, and find themselves, at fifteen, glowering up at nasty old authorities whose words they no longer trust, whose hypocrisy they no longer tolerate, whose purpose they no longer condone — how does one feel when one receives a D— on a Sophomore French II test? A D— on a test designed to "examine our capacity for managing the uses of pronouns and direct and indirect objects"? How exactly does one feel in this the age of dropouts, freakouts, moratoriums, debates over busing, and that diffusing, oozing uncertainty, and that "lack of identity" business that, like a heavy, itchy fabric has fallen down on students of all ages, suffocating and scratching them, and rendering them fish, heaped together in ragged, outworn nets? How exactly does one feel when one's paper comes back loaded to the very edges with *la*'s and *le*'s, *celui*'s, *elle*'s, *il*'s, *ceci*'s and *celui-la*'s, and none seems to align appropriately with the sentences written in that absolutely impossible language? How does one feel when an inability to come up with answers produces a test booklet displaying emptiness in the most frighteningly conspicuous places, like an eight-year-old boy with the largest tooth you ever saw sitting right up against the largest spaces you ever saw? How does one feel in this the exalted Age of Aquarius when one gets a D— on a French II exam on personal pronouns and direct and indirect objects? "I mean, does it even matter anymore, Marty?"

"I felt this high." Marty held her hand perfectly still, flat out, palm down, parallel to the ground, an inch above the top of her shiny loafers with the dull "lucky penny" stuffed into the little slit on the top of them. Those pennies are still worn to fetch, perhaps, the same luck we sought. "I could have crawled into my socks except they were too high. Poor grades do something to your ego. They make you feel so small and unimportant. Then I'm afraid . . . well, you know, what's really the worst, well, not really the worst, but you know, what's hardest, is that you kind of hate to show people how you feel. 'How'd you do, Marty?' 'Oh, so-so. All right, good enough. I didn't really study that hard.' You know. You just don't rush down the halls yelling, 'Hey, you guys, I got a D—! I got a D—! Aren't you proud of me? I'm living up to your expectations.'

"Then I know I have to tell Mother and Daddy. He seems to take it easier. Mom is harder. She just can't understand why I'm not doing better. Maybe I should say, why I'm not smarter. We all know I'm no genius. But of course I don't always get D—'s. I get B's and C's. Teddy's going to be real smart though. He's only in fifth grade but you can tell already. His teacher told Mom he's going to be real smart. I'm glad in a way, that he's got the brains in the family. It's more important for men to be smart than women. I can always get a job or, well . . . someday I'll have a husband. But Teddy, men have to make money and they have to be brainy to do that.

"Actually we're just like Mom and Dad. I look like Mom and Teddy's got Daddy's brains. Teddy's going to be a doctor, I'll bet. Daddy never says anything about it but once I heard him talking on the phone to Uncle Phil. Phil's my mother's brother. And he said something about the real Dr. Ballam, or waiting for the real Dr. Ballam to take care of him. I felt that, like, well, maybe he didn't really care what happens to me just as long as I look pretty. He loves it when I cook, for example. He and Mother act like a king and queen. I cook and Teddy waits on them. We don't do this very often because I have homework. That's the lousy part. Every night during the week and Sunday, too, they all get to watch television but Marty has to go upstairs and do her homework. Dad lets me watch like maybe one hour on school nights. He never believes it when I tell them I'm finished. He probably would if I started to get good grades. Pretty soon Teddy will start having homework and he won't be able to watch either, that little rat.

"I suppose Dad's doing the best thing. He works hard for us. He wants us to have good lives and to be happy. He always says, 'If I have one wish in life, it's that I know that you and Teddy and your Mother are safe, happy, and well-protected.' You met Daddy. Didn't you like him? He was much better-looking when he had hair. You should see the photographs of him when they got married."

"As good as Dr. Abelson . . . ?"

"No, not really. But don't tell him I said that. Promise?"

"Promise."

Three days after graduating from pharmacy school, Martin Arnold Ballam quit his job at Simeon Drugs where for years he had worked, first in the stock room, then as a delivery boy, and finally, in his last years of school, as a sales clerk.

"Those jobs, as much as I hated doing everything, except the selling part, kept me alive. They had a funny system in those days. When you came they gave you a job where you couldn't see the customers and they couldn't see you. Now they call them consumers, but in those days they were still customers. Anyway, then when you got better and had some experience, they'd change your job to delivery. Then you'd see the customer but not in the store, you see. By the time I was finishing with school they let me do a little selling. For a while there I was making more money as a salesman than I did as a pharmacist later on. As soon as I became a pharmacist, 'course I moved to a different place then, but anyway, what with the expenses of being married — I got married exactly one week after graduating. We didn't have much money. Marjorie, Mrs. Ballam, she worked with this sewing machine outfit. What the hell was their name?"

"Singer?"

"No. I know Singer; this was a small outfit. They ran a business in Columbus and Indianapolis and here. Well, in those days, no one else had money, but we had a little. Finally things worked out. We lived in an apartment in a building right around the corner from here. Just last month here they tore it down. They're going to build one of those apartment spreads with stores in the bottom. The whole thing. Marjorie and I took the kids to see the place. Funny, that place had, well, really, if you want to be precise, it had what they called two and a half rooms. The smallest bedroom and the tiniest kitchen. Lucky for us it was that small though. I don't think we had three pieces of furniture to our name in those days.

"Funny how things change. You know, really, I knew things were going to work out just about as they have. I mean, really, I just knew somehow we'd stick it out and someday we would be living in a nice home. You've been in our home. It's a nice home. Nothing special, no castle. It ain't no Camp David or Onassis, but it's got all you really need. Modern kitchen and all. I've got a beautiful basement, stays dry as a bone.

"But what I wanted to tell you, I just knew like Goldwater said, remember, in my heart, it was going to work out just about like it did. Some guys worry themselves sick about it. Marjorie and I didn't even talk about it. We just knew. Maybe I read it in a horoscope somewhere like Marty and her mother read every day. I've always worked in the pharmacy and drug business, and of course it just had to get bigger. So now, like the story says, I manage this whole affair. Still, you know, it's funny to see that apartment come down. It's like, you know, a bit of your life taken away from you. Even though you still have better things and you wouldn't want to go back to those times for a million bucks, there's still a part of you, like they say, that comes down with all the brick and wood and plaster. You've been talking to Marty a lot, eh?"

Marty and Marjorie Clausen Ballam are more than a bit proud of the head of their household. They speak of him often, never sanctimoniously, as thoughts of him return and return again in their reflections on life, its meanings, or just simply in the day-to-day processes which, after all, constitute one's own private identity, as well as one's grasp of the entire world. Both wonder where they might have been if it weren't for him, or where other marriages, other matches, or an impetuous step might have taken them.

Frequently, but on weekend evenings especially, this one handsome and strong mother, her sleeves folded back, a clip-on apron embracing her middle, sits across the kitchen table from the daughter who everyone would agree resembles her, and against a silence broken only by the soft grinding purr of the kitchen clock they dream aloud and to themselves of men and women together and alone, of families, and of all sorts of marvelous futures which, like trays of Christmas cookies, are spread out before them over the counters and tables of their working spaces. They think, too, about means, finances, money, bills, and balanced bank statements or allowances which properly saved or smartly invested might even take them to New York, or California, or Hawaii; Australia, Paris, London, Singapore, or Mexico. They imagine the world's majestic, rich, and glamorous ladies: "Jackie," Elizabeth Taylor, Princess Grace, the Queen of England, Rose Kennedy. And they speak in tones of sober maturity and reasoned daring of possessing great, great wealth. Their voices dropping, the room's light dimming, they share a fantasy of limitless resources, virtual wells of resources and constant replenishment.

"You know the kind," Marty will say, "with slaves carrying you around and four cars in the garage. You know like that ad on TV where the man has nothing to do so he keeps pushing his car over the cliff. And then he and his chauffeur walk back to his mansion and inspect all the rest of his cars?" Wealth would bring bushels and bushels of new shoes and gloves and purses, and closets with so many dresses they would have to be filed by some complicated sorting system.

"No, you know what they'd do? They'd computerize all your clothes for you. Then you could push a button telling what kind of dress you'd want and there would be those revolving clothes racks like at the cleaners. Then the dress would appear. Plop."

But so often their thoughts, their night dreams aloud, are swished silent and motionless by an interrupting sense of communal allegiance and thankfulness. Then they honor the man of the house, the rightful head, and together appeal to God, perhaps, to let him stay with them for a good long time, at least for a time beyond that which anyone dares to contemplate. They might also speak, in these rare moments in which time becomes the happy victim of sensuous flirtations with luxury, of the poverty they have seen not only in sections of their own town but in the ghetto neighborhoods of the large cities to the north and south which they can't help but observe from time to time when they ride the trains together as one single, substantial, and interlocked family.

"Seems like they always build the tracks right along those poor people's houses. It must be terrible all that noise and dirt. That's what's nice about airplanes. It's all so clean, and you come down in such lovely areas." Marjorie Ballam.

"My social studies teacher once told us that whenever we take the train we should be very careful to watch for the different regions of the city. Like the slums and the business districts and the residential districts. You really can learn quite a lot just by riding the trains. Planes are faster, but you don't get to see anything. But I like them better." Marty Ballam.

By anyone's standards, the homes around Michigan Street are comfortable, lovely, "as much as anyone needs." Always a bit of space shows between the houses as well as between the house fronts and the street. Always a bit of space. Address numbers are clearly marked and shortened driveways or concrete runners make it possible to park an extra car or two. Usually a screened-in porch pokes out from the front of the house, and often, too, old-fashioned, double-seat swings are visible, suspended from the plank-board ceilings, a bicycle or two leaning behind them, and firewood stacked, waiting for winter, behind them. The porches and swings are first to feel the seasons change. The thin, bamboo-textured shades tacked on to creaky rollers, wound up above the window openings, collect the frost. It's easier just to pull them down during the winter in order to keep the snow off the porch than it would be to replace the screens with windows, which because of their size would be terribly costly, not to mention heavy. The rest of the windows in the houses typically have aluminum sliding storm windows and screens all part of one single assembly. They make the winterizing of houses simple and quick. And just as simply, the houses change back, opening themselves to the sun, breathing deeply again, and welcoming the spring and summer.

"All you do," Martin Ballam was saying as he crouched beneath the large window on the stair landing between the first and second floors, "is pinch in these two little fellows here and that releases the . . . come on baby . . . that's it . . . then you push it up to the top, a little farther, as high as it will go. There. Like that. Now the other window comes down. Pinch the things. They always stick. I just can't get them . . . they work so goddamn well when they're new. There it is. Easy as that! So! I often think it would be nice if everyone in America could live in a house like this. You don't need more space. You don't need more than this. Those big houses with all that ground are just a headache. You got to have twenty men working for you just to keep your house up. You can have that! Me, I'll take this.

"I'm going to tell you something which you don't have to believe. If today, right this minute, a guy came to the door and says 'Ballam, on the spot, I'll give you forty thousand dollars for your place, lock, stock and barrel,' you know what I'd do? I'd laugh in his face. Where am I going to get something as good as this for forty, for fifty thousand dollars? You know the way they build buildings today? You know what that junk is made of? I'd like to see everyone in a home like this. Maybe a little smaller, maybe a little larger. It'd be very nice. Don't get me wrong. I don't mean tract houses, like when you come in drunk and you end up in your neighbor's place 'cause they all look so damn much alike. That's a goddamn funny thought, though, you know? You have this guy staggering out of his car and going in this house, waking up the next day surrounded by people he's never even seen before. He's looking at them. They're looking at him. Didn't Carol Burnett do an act like that one night? Maybe, it was Dick Van Dyke? No, I think it *was* Carol Burnett.

"I'll tell you something else. I wouldn't mind a bit who moved into this neighborhood. Black, white, green, blue, yellow, red. If a man's got the money, he's got the right to buy whatever he wants. We got colored people living right around the corner. Right over here on . . . a . . . what's its name . . . on . . . Wayland Place. Right over here on Wayland. You wouldn't want to meet finer people. They got a daughter who goes to school with Marty, they're in the same class. No problems at all. Marjorie always says she wishes some of our white friends were as nice. Were as polite."

Passing the Danforth family's house on Wayland Place on their way to school is by now rather routine for Marty and Teddy Ballam. When the Danforths moved there — "Was it one, two, three years ago already? Where does the time disappear to?" — Marty still accompanied her younger brother, this despite his protestations and his desire to pick up as many leaves as he could carry in the fall, or to make mounds of diminutive snowballs with his heavily mittened hands in the winter. They would trudge along slowly, she bundled up in high boots and a navy pea coat, he with a six-foot muffler of even, wide blue-and-gold striping wrapped what seemed to him hundreds of times around his neck and shoulders. Then, as in a loyalty to ritual, he would stoop to examine a stone or wrapper and she would yank at him to continue. Twenty little steps further on, humming a child's score, he would find a newly shoveled driveway which would mean sweet, fresh snow; or in the autumn he would find raked heaps of crisp and satin leaves. Then of course, as is the reasoned way, he would have to bolt from her unexpectedly and with a charging whoop settle bottom first on the soft pile. And together Teddy and the leaves would crackle with unexpected delight.

Marty came to hate it. At twelve and thirteen it was kind of fun, actually, to show off your baby brother. She could almost use him, especially when there were older boys around. It seemed to her that Teddy ignited a sort of fantasy in them of playing mother and father. They would come to treat him like their own son, then act, in that wondrous way, as parents themselves, even though it might only be the first time the young man had come around. Naturally, Teddy would ruin everything. Naturally. Not only the fantasy, but the way the fantasy helped these two others to find a means of moving together and avoid, in the beginning anyway, the honest sharing of private matters they might never have dreamed one shares "with a boy!" Or, with a girl!

"Stop acting like Mom and Dad," Teddy would scream at them. Maybe, too, he would even cry or run from the room seeking either of his parents and through them some vestige of justice. Marty and her friend would laugh, as parents laugh, although they felt some shame as well.

In those early September days three or four years ago, when the black family first arrived, and the thirty new black children were for the first time delivered to the school in the large, yellow buses with the wide black stripes down the side, Marty didn't mind so much when Teddy found something to do in front of the Danforth home. She would move nearer to the street and then halt, very casually. Watching her brother snatch at a squirrel running a hundred feet away, or stomp acorns under his heel, she would gaze unobtrusively over his head at the porch and windows of the Danforths' white house. It was, she so often mused, almost a carbon copy of her own home. The same front porch with the shades, although the Danforths did not have a swing, the same double-dormered roofs on either side and the identical crisscrossed window panes on the top floor. Did the Danforths have an attic with junk like theirs in it too? They even had a tree on the side of the house where she guessed the kitchen was located, exactly where the small maple she had helped to plant stood on their own property. It was kind of funny, "eerie" as Marty would say, this Danforth house filled with its special tingling mystery. Several times she tried to speak about it with Teddy as they trudged on to school.

"What do you think it's like in there?" she would ask her ward, who by now was totally camouflaged with leaves although he seemed unaware of it. "Do you think they have a dog or cat or something?"

"Where?"

"In there, in the Danforths'."

"Who are they? Do we know them? Hey, you're always telling me to come on. Now you're the one who isn't coming." But the mystery about the house remained for this young woman on her way, back and forth, five days a week to the junior high school. She thought about the house every day. She thought about it hard when she saw Susan Danforth in English or Social Studies class. What happens to Susan when she goes home? Maybe she gets all swallowed up in a big cave or a dark pit or something. Or maybe there are funny things hanging from the ceilings, or, I know, staircases leading to secret rooms and tunnels.

"Then again, I used to think if the house is so much like ours on the outside, maybe they're the same on the inside too. So you know what I did? I decided that the best way for me to see the inside was to wait for Halloween and then I'd take Teddy trick or treating. He really comes in handy sometimes. That's what I did. When I think of it now it's so embarrassing, but you wouldn't believe how we all used to wonder about it. Everyone used to talk about it all the time. You know. We knew it was just like all of our homes. Someone even said he'd watched Mr. and Mrs. Danforth move their furniture inside. But, I don't know, I still had to see for myself. After I did it, I felt like a fool. Then I wanted to get one last peek so I planned to take Teddy home again and change his costume so we could go there again. I stopped 'cause I began to feel that Mrs. Danforth was either going to call my mother at that point, or the men in the white coats would be coming for me."

All of that "silliness" ended several years ago. A hundred years ago as far as Marty was concerned. For now, eons later, the walk by the Danforths' en route to the senior high school only occasionally brings forth memories of those first autumn days, that one peculiar Halloween night, the sense of eerie craziness, and through it all, Teddy's ingenuousness and impeccable lack of comprehension.

"You know I often wonder whether people have the same thoughts that I have. Like whether Teddy ever knew what I was thinking. We talk now a little about the Negroes; there are some in his class. But I wonder whether other people have those crazy thoughts. Like, you know, on Stapleton Avenue where we walked that other time, there's that fence, remember, that long white picket fence, and I let my purse rattle on it? You know why I do that? It seems so silly to even talk about it. I once saw a movie where the girl always walked to school. I think she was in college, and she used to do it, or something like it. So I do it, not because I like the sound especially, but it's kind of like I'm a movie star. I pretend there are lots of cameras and lights and people and things in the street and they're watching me do this scene. Oh, and it's all going to be very romantic. I'll meet some boy and then we'll walk by the gate together. It's all silly isn't it?

"Once my Aunt Lorraine — she isn't really my aunt, she's a friend of my mother's, they always go shopping together. They used to play cards or something, and they got married at the same time and all that. Anyway, she came by on Stapleton and I was actually talking to myself. Out loud. Like a nut. I was in the movies and talking away like I was going to the funny farm. I was so embarrassed, and she thought I was absolutely out of my mind. You should have seen her. She looked like she was going to faint right in the middle of the street. So you know what I said? I said something like, 'Oh, I'm sorry Aunt Lorraine. I saw you coming, but I've got a test in English and I had to memorize a big speech from this play. I keep thinking I'm going to forget it.' And I went on and on like this and she actually believed me. I think.

"Sometimes I think that I can't tell lies without being caught at it.

Once I lied to my father. It was so embarrassing. He knew darn well I was lying but he never said a thing. Never once. It had something to do with money. It would have been better if he did say something. I felt that big. But sometimes, too, I feel that I could tell really important lies and get away with it, like that time with Lorraine. I mean, you know, really big lies, like about crimes and murders. Sometimes I imagine I've killed someone. No one has seen me do it. I'm the only one in the world who knows I did it. Then all sorts of strange little people question me, and I look them right in the eyes and lie between my teeth. I even fool the lie detector by keeping real great control over my breathing and heart. I just sit there perfectly still. Sometimes this happens in my dreams. It's a lot stranger there, but it's like the same thing. I know something or I've done something and people are asking me and I'm lying and they're taking it all in. They believe every word I say. Is this normal? You didn't believe me when I told you 'the men in the white suits are going to be coming for me any day now.' If they see you with me, they'll take you too."

Later in the fall of her sophomore year, with the trees bare of leaves and the earth bracing once again for the winter's first snows and long frost, Marty and Mike Arnenstein went out together. It was at night. Marty passed it off as a date, but Teddy "damn him," insisted on calling it "an affair." With Mike waiting on the porch, clapping his hands together to keep them warm, Teddy ran around the living room jabbering things like, "Marty's getting married," "Mike and Marty," and all sorts of greetings about loving and kissing.

"Mother, make him stop it already." Then to Teddy: "I'll get you for this."

"Teddy come upstairs. Come upstairs. I want to show you something. Come upstairs, now. Right now. This instant, young man. Come home early, Marty. Have a good time at the movies." Then together they walk to the Century Theater about ten blocks away, talking a lot about schools, grades, Mrs. Gralie's stupid tests, and the dress that Miss Donovan wears every Monday, Wednesday, and Friday without fail, and Mr. Langton's combing his hair downward over his forehead in order to cover up the baldness, and Mr. Belden, the gym teacher who is so tough even the police force would probably reject him.

"I hate that man with a passion."

"He's a bummer."

"Becky says if he bothers her once more in the halls about anything she's going to stab him with a scissors."

"Then we could drag him into the furnace and the whole school would stink."

"The whole city would smell. Ugh. He's such a horrible man. Why do they keep him?"

"I don't know. Somebody must like him. He's probably old man Harney's right-hand man."

"I don't like *him* either. You can't trust him for a second. He'll tell you one thing one moment, and say something entirely different the next. I know some teachers that don't like him either. Sometimes they'll tell you."

"He's really a bastard. My dad's got stories about him. He's just lucky to keep that job of his."

"Why don't they fire him?"

"I guess the school board likes him too much."

"Hmmm."

And there is college to talk about, and jobs, the importance of getting good grades right from the beginning, the fear that junior high marks might already be hurting their chances, the fact that extra-curricular activities really make a difference, and "things like that." But they speak as well of their animosity toward some of the older kids in the high school, like Mike's brother's former best friend Stephen Mackler, "who used to be such a nice guy but who now is a hippie with beads and all that, smoking marijuana and thinking he is really something big. You can't believe it, Marty, he used to be the greatest guy."

Mike told Marty that his father said that "all this business of blaming this marijuana on the parents is ridiculous. Something just went wrong with Steve's brain. It's as simple as that! Just like people suddenly go crazy or jump off a building or get a gun and think they can just go out and shoot all the goddamn people in the world. Something goes woof, like that, in their brains, and you got to lock them up. You lock them up for their sake as well as for innocent people just walking around like you and me."

"Between you and I," Mr. Arnenstein had said, walking home from a Saturday morning high school football game that autumn, "when I see these kids playing football and marching in the band, I feel proud of each and every one. Like Mike's friend Marty. You know her. Now there's a perfectly wonderful girl. If I could, if I had the power in my hands, I wouldn't change a hair on that girl's head. She's a wonderful girl. Wonderful girl. But if you've ever seen these others with the hair down to here and without the shoes. Thirty degrees outside, they're walking around without the shoes, without the coats, without gloves. They're nuts. If this is supposed to be cute, or rebellion, or hate the establishment . . . I think they're nuts.

"But I'll tell you something as long as you're so interested in them. The parents who make such a fuss about them and say how dangerous it is that long hair and bare feet are walking around under their perfect children? They're nuts too. Believe me. They're just as nuts. People should let people alone. A man with a gun, that's one thing. I'm not talking about that. But a bunch of rich kids who want to look poor, who they hurting? Themselves! It's nobody's business. They want to catch pneumonia and die, let 'em catch pneumonia and die." Stephen Mackler was free to walk with "them."

Coming out of the movie, Mike and Marty walked quite a while before the talk came freely to them, before the talk, as it were, came back. Walking almost a full block in silence, they peered in the small shop windows on Burlington Avenue, watching with fascination the breath steaming from their lips, then disappearing into the night and the sky toward the moon they had agreed could no longer be the same.

"You want to go to a party?"

"Sure. Where?"

"Buddy Wilmick's sister's house. Near you. You know. A whole bunch of kids are going."

"What time is it?"

"Ah . . . nine-thirty."

"O.K. But, I'm going to have to get home pretty soon."

"Sure. All right. We'll make it."

The walk to the party takes these two friends past the Ballam house, where Marty, walking to the inside of Mike, just as they had learned once somewhere, dares to peek through the windows at the dancing gray and white shafts, the metallic lights of television. A casual glance, unnoticed certainly. But for an instant, a time which as it happens seems so long and so reluctantly urged into a memory and no more, the wish to end the date right then, and be home again with her parents and the glow within, explodes. In that instant, the wish explodes so loudly it must be heard by all the world, but surely by him. Then, still in that same enduring instant, the wish disappears. But where? Into the sky, into memory, into a later instant? Maybe all three. Maybe so.

"Sometimes at night I feel so frightened. It's hard to say really, what I feel. I don't feel it every night of course. But like that night with Mike that I told you about. I don't know. It was like I was scared of something. Sometimes I feel I know what's going to happen in the future, like what was going to be happening at the party but . . . I don't know, I just get scared.

"You know what it's like? It's like — you're going to laugh at this — it's like when I know my period is coming soon. First any day now, and then any hour, and any second. I'm always convinced it's going to come in bed. Or sometimes I'll be talking in class and I'll think, I'll bet I get the curse right now. Janet and I used to talk about it a lot. She said she wasn't really scared but it — no that's not it. Someone told her once that when you're very late it means you might be pregnant, but when you're late but not *very* late, it means you almost were pregnant. It's like a warning or something like that. Last year we went and asked the nurse at school about it and she said that there were a lot of stories about getting your period and that girls ought to know if there is any reason for them to be pregnant. No. Is that right? I can't remember. She said: 'Janet, Marty, no one can tell you that you are pregnant without you knowing first.' Then she looked at us as if maybe we were pregnant. She asked whether we had something to tell her. I thought I'd die on the spot.

"Want to know how silly I was once. When I was about twelve or thirteen, there was this big picnic, and everybody messed around and ate near this lake. Then a bunch of kids went swimming. You know. And a whole group of guys came along and they dunked the girls and all that. That was kind of fun. Really. Then they started doing these things where, you know, the guy lifts the girl on his shoulders, and you try to pull the other girl over the guy's shoulder."

"Cockfighting."

"Is that what they call it? Well, before they started, I heard these guys talking about let's have some whatever-you-call-it fights cause it's 'the cheapest feel in town.' They're right too. By the time you get up on the guy's shoulders he's put his hands all over you. And these other girls thought it was just so great. I thought it was sickening what they were doing. I even told this one awful boy who kept pestering me to take his hands off or I'd call my father. Do you believe that? I actually said I'd call my father. These kids couldn't believe it. They looked at me like I was nuts. I felt like, remember when I told you about the time I lied to my father. That's how I felt. I wanted to drown on the spot."

Sandra Wilnick's party that one winter night had been wild. "Damn, it's really wild, huh, Marty?" Almost like a television drama's conception of what parties are like, is the way it was at Sandra Wilnick's house on, "I can't even remember the name of the street now. Oh, wow!" The rock records, and the throngs of people pushing and being pushed, and everyone loving it all. To walk by someone meant to touch them and be touched all over. And there were smells, familiar, but heavy and exaggerated. Young people and older people were there, yelling, whispering, mouths so close to ears, hands so close to hands, and Mike seeming so tall suddenly, and more, so old. What was worse than that was the girl so young, moving about, thanking her youth and two special parents, and praying she might never mature at all, or that she might bypass the entire clump of years out there in the living room, or stay forever exactly where she was a few moments ago.

In a room beyond the entrance hall, on top of a pile of coats, the lights aglow, a couple is making out, and with horror Marty recognizes Janet. "I mean, you know, it was all right for her to be doing that but I always thought . . . I mean . . . this all must sound so perverse. God, it sounds like a novel."

Six months later, now in the heat of the summer months, Marty Ballam, nicknamed after the man she had resembled so strongly during childhood, reminisces about that party and her inexplicable feelings of fear and forewarning. "That horrible den of iniquity. All I could think about was coming home and getting into a hot bath. It's so dumb really when you think of it. I wasn't born yesterday. But seeing Janet. She looked like she was being murdered. Once I walked in on a cousin of mine. She was baby-sitting for Teddy and me. I must have been about ten or something. And she was making out with her boyfriend on the couch and I giggled. I ran up the stairs and jumped on my bed and bounced up and down and giggled. I wasn't even embarrassed about it. I sound like a real prude, don't I? I'm not really, at least I don't think I am."

What comes out of these moments of talk and reminiscences is precisely that question: how does one know if he or she is a prude? What comes out is how one learns what almost amounts to hard sociological data, about sex, about making out, about potency and impotency, about beauty and ugliness. Each of us carrying on that drive to be this much bigger, that much smaller, this much ahead or that much behind the next one, and then the one after him. What comes out of these moments is how one learns that he or she is doing all right, what in fact is "all right"; and how what is "supposed" to be happening at fifteen hasn't already happened at twelve and therefore should have, or won't happen until seventeen and should have way before then. What comes out is how one is supposed to know even when she cannot confess to the fright and nausea and physical illness lasting until the following Tuesday when she can go back to Janet and lie. It comes out because, fed by that one enduring instant, none of the memory has gone away.

"Were you sick, Marty? I was going to call you last night to see if you needed something, but then Billy called and I think that stupid thing is on again."

"No. I just had you know what. I had such unbelievable cramps, I thought I was either going to die or give birth right on the spot to some monster."

"Oh, I know, don't remind me. Hey, there's going to be a groovy party Saturday night . . ." And they're off again, their physiologies no longer charging them or running them or being them, but rather, racing to keep up, and never daring for a moment to break down or protest for respite.

"Sometimes I run around so much I feel like I'm never ever going to get sleepy. Crazy isn't it? I'll probably drop dead at thirty with a heart attack and I won't even know it." But everything else is left so far behind; that last weekend, and most especially last weekend's date when "everyone was making out like mad, you should've see them, Marty, oh, wow!" is either forgotten in the rush of new plans and fresh intentions, or stuffed like stained laundry into the bottom of a hamper where it is buried alive in the mess of yesterday's and last winter's. Who after all, in times like these, admits to fear or to a sense of empty inadequacy? At this precise and ecstatic instant, confession surely begets banishment, so you bolt on, blame it on the cramps, and borrow just enough from a culture which has itself come far enough (that is to say, really, not far enough) that the packets of fear and insecurity come to be saved for, and described for you by psychiatrists, counselors, and cadres of "trained professionals."

All of life, just about, is coming to be seen by some of us as a series of packets, of television shows, of denials followed instantaneously by dramatic presentations and unadulterated pretense. Tab A is put into slot A and night follows day. Tab B is put into slot C and before your eyes is enacted the dissolution of a language and a history you had not only depended on, you had by fifteen years of age come to believe were the only language and the only history there ever were and ever would be. Certainly they were the only worthwhile language and history. Who could contest that? Those silly German, Latin, Spanish, French, and Russian teachers with their posters and photographs, marked-up short stories and novellas, and everything printed on that cheap, foreign paper with the uncut pages.

Walk past the vaporous silvers and purples of television and the warmth of a home, the model her father had wished everyone might own, and the three of them sitting inside like dumb fools, like immaculate saints, and step from the cold into an oozy, textured warmth. Then at last innocently insert tab C into slot C and watch them collide. Molecular people in the most prime of all prime time. Watch her, Janet, from English and French and Social Studies and from after school and weekends and telephone calls, and from the showers after P.E., and from all those intimate eons, watch her bent backward on that pile of coats and gloves and scarves, her skirt half off, and "the funny little design on her pants so visible, so close and touchable," that it keeps you home in your own bed for two more days.

"'You're just out of it, Marty. If you don't realize that stuff's going on, man, you're really out of it. You ought to keep your eyes open once in a while. What the hell do you think school is all about anyway?' That's kind of what Mike told me. He thought I was a child. I wouldn't dare for a million dollars tell him that I had spoken to my mother about some of the things at that party. And I was glad I didn't have another date with him that following weekend. I don't think I could have stood it. I trusted Mike. We once agreed that it was a good idea that kids shouldn't smoke and that we'd tell our parents if we smoked. Or drank. And we talked about how far, you know, you should go with a girl. And he agreed that you can pet and all that, but that, well, you know, the rest can wait 'til marriage. He agreed and I thought he was just great. What a sucker.

"Then, I don't know, something happens to boys. They all get together and do whatever they do and ride around and all that, and they decide that you can't be a big man until you sleep with a girl, or lots of different girls. I'd like to know what he'd say. I wish you'd ask him if he wants his wife to be a virgin. I'll bet he says yes. Oh, I don't care what he says. I was such a fool to trust him. He probably thinks I'm some kind of a basket case walking around wishing sex hadn't been invented. Maybe girls are the same way. Who knows. Who cares."

Most of the conversations of those three cherished summer months came around to the same themes: boys and sex, popularity, clothes and appearance. But it is almost as if the language itself contained pockets of feelings often having nothing whatever to do with what was being spoken about or, for that matter, with the feelings that popped up here and there: the anxiety with the willingness, the fear with the daring, the reservations with the plotting. At some level we know so well about these pockets because we have put them there ourselves, hoping perhaps that someone else might find them and might speak of them and to them.

"You really have to get to know someone a long time before you know what he's thinking," Marty said once. "Even when they say one thing, they might be thinking or wishing something entirely different. Did you know that? Oh sure you do. That's why you're a psychologist, or social . . . or whatever you are. I always think that's really the way I want my husband to be. He should be able to tell when I'm saying one thing and meaning it, or saying something else and meaning something different. You know what I mean? 'Course, he's got to be good-looking, too."

"Naturally."

"Naturally."

"Like William, maybe?"

"Well . . . I . . ."

"Just a little?"

"I guess more than a little."

William Garrison Rinehart had come from out of the blue early that September, absolutely brand new. Before then, he simply never was. But on September sixth at precisely 4:30 P.M. he was among the living, socially born. Mr. Ballam had introduced them at the drugstore and, "Oh wow! He looks just like that ad. You know the one? 'I came back.' Before I left the store that time I whispered to Daddy something like, 'you sneaky man,' and he blushed. You should have seen him." William Garrison Rinehart. He couldn't have come at a better time. Surely God-sent. Just what the doctor ordered. Just what the horoscope predicted. "Do you believe that? Unbelievable. All true. All true. I kid you not!"

The time, or the sense of time of fifteen-year-olds, can anyone describe it or feel it again? Are we ever able to know just how it is that eight months can "zing" by so quickly, and yet, at the very same time, crunch along so slowly? Is the experience of that special time identical to how we perceived it immediately in retrospect, that is, at the moment when that eight-month period concluded? And is that immediately retrospective calculation the same as when we look again, in retrospect, but from a time, say two, three, five years hence? Naturally, it's not really the same, but is it close? Is it now at all like it was, and does everyone think about time this way? In other ways? What really do we remember of school? Of how slowly or quickly this part or that part passed? Or is it, maybe, that we recall the time of the recollection, the feeling of time moving quickly or slowly, rather than the actual events that filled all that time? Or is it not this either?

William Garrison Rinehart. He had, in fact, helped along the very time, the very adolescence of a young woman. He didn't start time moving again as some will say. How foolish. Time was moving. "My life came alive. You can't say that. Can you say he made life come alive?" A private, totally personal time was clicking off its markers again. It was in her eyes, in that appearance the girls spoke so much of, and in the dance that was her motion around the house. The lights and cameras and stardom followed her about.

But in the corridors of time, in and among its narrow slits and on its generous and expansive plains were also tucked away eight months almost exactly from the time of the party and the wish to return home. Then the two days in bed — the wish fulfilled perhaps — with what it seems so many young people diagnose as trauma. (How the word often sounds more deadly than the events it describes!) Those eight months were there too, deep inside time's pockets. The descriptions of life — the accounting, the reporting, the confessing that comprise a diary — contain all sorts of these pockets. Some stretching from Monday 'til Friday: "Thank God for Friday afternoons." Others from Friday until just as late as one dares stretch it on Sunday night: "Why don't they make us go to school on the weekends and let us stay home the rest of the time? Or better yet send our parents to school and let *us* stay home." Then the pockets of months and seasons, autumn or football and summers: "God, I wish we lived in California. But then I'd never see snow again and I love the snow, too. I would miss it, I'm sure."

William Garrison Rinehart. Tall and rich. Handsome. Publicly gruff, privately gentle. "He's conceited, but who cares! All men are, really. But he's earned the right. Even Jan is envious."

Like a wondrous revolving disc the seasons turn, and in the astrological space given over to September and October sits school, more Friday night dates, and more locker by locker conversations. There's the time they try to petition the school to permit them to wear pants. Certain they will lose, they sneak their skirts into their lockers, and when Mrs. Minelli, "that old fish," orders them to change back into "clothes" or go home, they march to the lav to resume their uniforms and talk about socks and stockings and panty hose and mini-dresses and maxi-coats. They speak about the boys too, of course, who helped them with their pants crusade, and, even more, about the boys for whom in part the crusade was launched.

But even these conversations, as animated and absorbing as they seem, remain but fillers. Fillers between weekends, between football games and, for Janet, cheerleading practices. For Marty, classes drone on. Time is homogeneous, a hunk, or maybe school has finally stopped it altogether. Nothing seems vital, nothing important. "I always get this funny feeling when I leave school and see the Negro kids piling into their buses, I should say bus. I always wonder what they get out of school, or like, do they date. They don't come to our parties but they probably have their own parties. They're probably better. It really seems a bit silly but you don't know what to say to them.

"Sometimes they frighten me. Like this morning I saw a whole bunch of guys walking down the hall. They seemed to be looking for a fight or something. I mean, they kind of walked like they owned the place. Actually, I knew one of the boys. He's in my English class. We talk a lot together after class, but when he gets in with his friends he acts tough and important. I don't say anything. I mean, I'm sure they know what they're doing. Sometimes when they're all together and talking very fast I don't even understand them. I used to think they did that just to bother us and that they couldn't even understand each other either. They just did it to annoy us. Like when Teddy was real little, my girlfriend and I, you don't know her, she moved away, we used to speak this crazy, make-believe language. Teddy would think we were talking about something. He'd get furious and start to cry or call for Mother and we'd die. That's what I think, used to think when I heard those kids. But they *are* talking. They can talk like us, but outside class they talk that other way. Fast and all that. It's like they're foreigners.

"Oh, you know what I dreamed once. I dreamed that . . . well, I have to tell you something before you can understand. There's this boy in Social Studies. He's a Negro and his name is Calvin . . . Calvin Marks . . . no, it's not Marks, it's something like that. Anyway, he's on the football team. He's a great athlete. Basketball, baseball, and everything. Well, he always wears these tight pants. Every time he moves you can see all his muscles move like right through his pants. The funny part is that I knew I always watched him especially when he wore these orange, they're . . . they're, pumpkin-colored pants. It was like he was naked. I used to wonder what would happen if anyone ever knew I was watching him. Can't you just see it: Marty Ballam, sex maniac, carried screaming from Social Studies class. So anyway, one day in the locker room some girls are talking about boys' clothes and how they like to go to the football games because the boys' pants are so tight. And I'm just bursting. I'm going to explode. And Jane what's-her-face says, 'Do you guys know Calvin Mingus?' Mingus, that's his name. 'Do you know Calvin Mingus?' And she goes into this thing about Calvin in Social Studies class with his green and orange pants. Oh wow! It was really wild! Just about every girl had noticed him and everyone was so surprised that everyone else had too. We just died laughing. I love that part.

"Oh, I almost forgot, the dream. I don't remember when I dreamed this but I was in Social Studies class and Calvin came in — this is part of the dream now — and said that he had heard all about our discussion in the lav about him and his pants. So what he wanted me to do was sit on his lap so I could feel his pants. I told him something like I really didn't want to, but I really did. And he said, 'Oh sure you do. Come up here little girl and sit on old Calvin's nice old lap.' And I wanted to. Then he said, 'You sit up here this minute or I'll come over there and murder you. Very slowly like, too.' I told you, I'm ready for the men in the white coats."

A funny feeling overtakes one, or maybe it just slips through one's adult defensiveness, when the meetings and walks with Marty and the kitchen conferences around the white formica table with all the Ballams assembled continue into a second year. The feeling has to do not so much with the increasing fuzziness of the distinction between friendship needs and "research requirements," as with being implicated in a sense of drama or dramatic occurrence that one wishes might soon come to pass. Rather suddenly we want life to take a magnificent turn in a direction no compass would ever comprehend, no astronaut be able to retrace. As silly as it sounds, we want people who are close but not really, how does one say it, honestly close, to become rich and famous. Maybe they could become movie stars, western heroes, great ladies of the world. Through some combination of their words and our words we want all of us who have shared the movies and parties and walks by a black family's home to become special and immortal. That's probably what it is: We wish to make the others and ourselves immortal.

"Maybe, who knows, we might live forever," Bill had told Marty one night as they rocked on the porch swing and, through their graceful motion together, transported themselves backward to the freest childhood and then forward again to a point in time where they dared look back at themselves and their own futures. "I know one thing for sure, I want to die before you."

"Oh no. I before you. You're the more important person."

"You're great."

"We're both important."

"Thank you. I think so too."

"That's nice."

"So are you."

And yet, the wish to bestow all of this immortality and specialness seems cruel in its condescension. Every poor black, "working-class" Catholic, Appalachian, Jew, has to make it upward to the top, higher than the top, then impossibly over the top to a place of absolution and sacredness. Nobel Prizes aren't even enough, and surely they're pretty close to immortality. Everyone is meant to be lifted up, higher, higher, just as a father swoops down and lifts his somewhat frightened child, the child with his father's eyes and his mother's manner, up into the smoky air, so that his back scrapes against the ceiling and the light gleams dangerous inches from his hair. Then the relief, the collapse of tension when the child is released, excused, and he sinks back, part way to the height of his father, their faces as close as faces dare be, a musical rest before the descent back to a child's height, and a child's topography. The child tottering, looks about, and that giant whose head surely would crash through all the ceilings of the world if he cared to raise himself to his fullest height, if, as they say on report cards, he ever extended himself to his fullest potential, straightens up. The moment catches its breath, then clicks on, the child down there, the adult up here.

That part of society down there, this part up here. And instantly, everyone is living in a house just like Martin Ballam's, like Mr. and Mrs. Danforth's too. Is that what it's all about? Maybe so. Part of it anyway, at least at this point.

But whose job is it to shovel away the condescension and uneasiness from partings and completions? Or should they remain, intended as they were? Who is supposed to say, "It's all right if we don't see one another as often as before," or "I'm as good as you, you're as good as me"? Who is to say, "We're both important"?

"So?"

"So what?"

"Will you write this up, all this stuff we talked about?"

"If I do I'll send it first thing to you and your parents so you can all check it over."

"Check it over for what?"

"Well, you know, there may be mistakes or things you don't want me to say."

"You don't have to do that. There's nothing you can say that wouldn't be all right."

"I wouldn't use your real name, of course."

"But you can. Why not? I don't have anything to hide. I really don't. I'm not ashamed of anything. Like remember when we talked about things like sex, or drugs, or marijuana, or politics. All those juicy little topics. I'm not ashamed of my feelings. A lot of kids feel like I do, so what's there to be ashamed of? That I don't get drunk or make out under the stairs of the boys' gym? I told you right at the beginning, remember? I told you we were just like everyone else, and that you weren't going to find anything interesting. Remember? That's what happened didn't it?"

"Hardly."

"You remember all that stuff about the fence and the movie camera with the lights and all that? You know why I do that? Look at me, I'm starting to analyze like you psychologists. Maybe that's what I'll be. A psychologist. Then I'll go around analyzing people like you do. Right?"

"Right."

"No. That fence thing. I think a lot about that. I know I'm not going to be any movie star. And I know that I'm never going to be anyone special. Not in the big world, or the little world either. I'm not going to be the President or famous or anything. If you wrote something about Nixon, that would matter, 'cause he's famous. He's somebody. He's, no, that's not what I really wanted to say. He's somebody but I'm somebody too, like Bill. But he's more important. I'm not that important or special. Like if he were killed, like President Kennedy, it would be horrible and everyone would know. But if I got killed, you know, my parents and my friends would be all shook up, but who would come? If I were young it'd make the papers and all that, especially if I got raped or murdered or something. But, well, you know.

"Hey, I've got a question for you," Marty resumed. "Just for once. If I got killed. I know. Really. Listen. If I got killed, what would you do? Would you feel sad?"

chapter six

the
golden
opportunity

*voluntary busing,
educational opportunities, and
desegregation*

busing for purposes of improving educational opportunities and for racial desegregation is undoubtedly one of education's most pressing issues. Interestingly, the actual experiences of the young people being bused across cities to grammar schools and high schools, as well as their attitudes toward busing, have proven to be of less interest than social scientific studies attempting to demonstrate the effects of various busing programs.

To learn about the reactions of students to busing, I rode school buses with black and Oriental students from Boston's inner city, and then spoke with white students in suburban schools. The conversations in chapter six reveal a few of the attitudes held by American students as busing continues to be an important political as well as educational point of controversy. The sophistication of these students is worth noting, as is their desire to be seen not as political units but as human beings.

The hours of riding a bus to and from school constitute a profound course in civics, sociology, or American history. Social change and political ideologies and campaigns reverberate in the lives of students who carry the load of desegregation inside and outside their homes and classrooms. The very word *busing* has ignited all sorts of conflicts and debates in the lives of many teachers, students, administrators, and parents. No one can assume the role of teacher without having thought seriously about the meanings and implications of busing. And yet, despite our knowledge and sensitivity, we must constantly remind ourselves that busing refers not to buses or to a political currency, but to the lives of human beings, young and old, and to the opportunities their culture holds out for them.

"A man's a fool to say anything truthful about busing these days," is what I heard someone say a few weeks ago. "You'll never prove anything to anyone. You take any bit of information and each side will use it as they want to," he continued. "It gets me though, that while you got a war going on, seems forever, with American boys dying every week and planes and helicopters being lost, that the people of this country would still be more upset over black kids sitting in their classrooms or using their toilets than they are about the war. I tell you, that's what I want to have explained to me."

These words, spoken by a fifty-year-old Boston man, made a great deal of sense to me. Since the inception of the Boston school busing program, Samuel Tavorsky has driven a bus for the city to several suburban towns, and in his way has come to learn more about the lives of the young black people involved with the program than most of us. Several years ago he had his doubts about the virtues of racially integrated schools. He did not like a lot of the students and believed, with many, that children belong in their own neighborhoods. Gradually, though, he found himself comparing the schools in the poverty areas of Boston with what he saw in the suburbs. Something very deep inside him was touched by these perceptions that marked the little study he was making, and his attitudes changed.

"It's not a bit fair," Sam reasoned aloud as we drove home in the old bus along with forty-five students. "Not a bit fair that these kids should suffer just because adults like you and me don't want to live with their families. If you ask me the whole thing stinks! They got just as much right getting the best education they can as my own kids. Yessir. As my own kids. You want to know what the trouble is? The trouble is that this country has it figured they always got to hate some group. So they pick blacks. You talk to anybody who's worked with black folks, they'll tell you same as I, they're just like you and me. Isn't a shred of difference between us. I know. Five years ago I started on this job, well, you knew me then. I wouldn't speak to any one of them." He motioned back over his shoulder in the direction of the students. "Didn't even like the idea that from time to time I had to touch them, you know, when they went at it. But I'll tell you. They've educated *me. I'm* the one learning from *them.* I want only the best for them. They deserve the chance. So do the kids we leave behind. They do too. They ought to penalize these schools that don't allow black children in. Orientals too. They ought to penalize 'em. Make 'em pay ten times as much. If these folks out here could see what I see every day they'd change. Believe me. Nerve of these people opposing busing. Making it such a big issue like they have. I tell you, they ought to penalize them plenty. Really stick it to 'em. Fellows like you that write ought to demand that they do. *You* know these kids. You aren't going to tell me you could find a nicer group of children anywhere. Am I right?"

"You are. You are."

"There you have it. That's all I'm talking about. Just as simple as that. These are damn good kids. When they have those hearings about busing why don't they call on *me?* I'd tell 'em what I know about these people and their families. I get a good look at this busing thing, you know. I see and hear what a lot of folks are saying. They ought to call me."

Samuel Tavorsky's method of inquiry into busing was in fact the same as my own. We listened and watched, Sam spending more time at it than I. We spoke, too, with many people: the riders, the hosts, their teachers, counselors, and various school administrators. Neither one of us could really be credited with conducting a complete piece of social science research, but the words we heard and the sights we witnessed made us, at least to each other, "experts" on the experiences of more than a few students. True, there would be many who would wonder why we even took the time to observe this busing enterprise unfold every day. Some people, in fact, have advised Sam that his job requires him to drive the students to school and return them to their homes each night, and that he should keep his mouth shut the rest of the time. Others have told me that my speaking with black students about their school experiences is an outrageously patronizing act. "The guy has no business speaking to black children," is the message I receive quite regularly. I've not yet been told this by the students I know, the ones who trust Sam as much as they do many of their teachers.

Sam Tavorsky and I share another quality. Neither of us seems to know, really, the hard facts of the Boston busing program. When someone utters the words *busing* or METCO (Metropolitan Council for Educational Opportunities), the organization which sponsors busing in our city, we both reflect on people, young people usually, but not always. I know that we both think almost automatically of Ronnie Harmwood from Dorchester, a tall, seventeen-year-old who wears the most handsome clothes I have ever seen, and whose experiences are as moving as any study that the professionals will underwrite. Without consulting Sam, I would bet that Ronnie's words would be among the first we would hear when someone mentions busing.

Riding in the bus one day after school, Ronnie, who was then fifteen, reported to us that he saw no one having problems in the METCO program. "Even the white folks don't mind us being there once the first push is over, if you know what I mean. I s'pose they got a right being angry having us come in, but they get used to it. It's a two-way deal. Everybody can see that. They got to get used to us, we got to get used to them. On a day-by-day basis. That's where the tension is. Some of 'em think all they got to do is get through one day and then we'll be out of there. They can't believe we're going to keep coming out. But it's working. No real problems that I can see."

I remember asking him about his educational plans and the sorts of experiences that he was encountering. I was more impatient than Sam, who spoke only when he felt the urge and then let the students respond. I wanted answers, ammunition perhaps, to counter those who constantly mount evidence to "prove" the undesirability of racial integration. So what if I *am* doing a study? I would say to myself. Why shouldn't young people like this man have their impressions count? "What's wrong with *their* voices?" I keep asking people who seek to know the "real truths" about busing.

"I'll tell you what METCO's done for me," Ronnie replied calmly.

"It's made a man of me. What do you think of that?" Like doting uncles, Sam and I grinned as the bus rumbled on. "I'm not saying this for you two guys. It's the God's truth. I wasn't doing anything in my old school that amounted to anything. Nothing. When I came out here I saw the world a whole different way. They care about us out here. I mean, they really want us to do good things. Like go to college. I got a lot of teachers I know are going to feel mighty fine when I get into college. You can't beat it. There isn't any way I'm going to fail unless I really screw up, but if I do it's going to be my doing, nobody else's."

"That's being a man," Sam said nodding his head up and down.

"Tell him, Sam," Ronnie went on. "That's being a man, all right. You get a better start out here, you know what I mean? I don't care about living out here, although if my mom wanted it I'd go with her. But that isn't what it's all about. When you live where I live you don't start where the others do. They're always ahead of you, 'cept for those kids who you grow up with. I went to school, you know, and messed around with those guys. All those years, I knew I was better than they were. Anyone could see that. But like, my mother used to say, that isn't where the real competition comes from. It's the white kids in Brookline, Newton, Lexington, Wellesley. Those are the competition. Ain't enough, she'd say, being better than the kids in the project. You got to start measuring yourself against all the kids in the world, 'least those around here."

I could hear Mrs. Harmwood's voice in the language of her oldest son. She had said almost the same thing to me. The school Ronnie now attended was the single most important part of the Harmwood family's life. "I'd steal for him," Margaret Harmwood exclaimed. "I'd get money any which way, 'cause that busing's the golden opportunity we've been waiting for. Folks go around talking about that one golden opportunity that God's got saved up for them. Half the time they don't even know they just had it fall in their laps. Getting him in that school's the golden opportunity. I got him there now, then I'll send my other three. Ernest's just about making a wreck of me already." She was smiling. "Says he wants to go too. I could send him to another place but I want my boys together on the bus going out there. I'll get them all in those schools and you'll see how it's going to change their lives.

"Well, now of course you know what's happening. They got all these people on one side yelling against the people on the other side, and in the meantime we're just supposed to sit and wait until they've all made their decisions about what *they* say *I* can do with my children. Well, I'm not waiting. I've had my golden opportunity and the good book says to take it when it comes 'cause it probably's only going to pass by once for this family."

"You see a big difference between METCO students and the white students, Ronnie?" I asked.

"No."

"No differences you can spot?"

"No."

"That's all you're going to say, huh?"

"What else you want me to say? We're black and yellow, they're white. The differences end there. They got smart kids, we got smart kids. They got popular kids, we got popular kids. Nothing's really integrated out there, but it doesn't mess up the schooling. We're learning, they're learning. All this stuff about us pulling them down's a lot of crap. It's just political jive. Whites don't want us, all they have to say is we're ruining their precious little children. They ought to know about ruining children too." His anger was building.

"Take it easy, son," Sam urged gently.

"I'm all right, Sam," Ronnie responded. "Just gets me though, that everybody's always wondering whether the white kids are being hurt. Look around in here, man, doesn't anyone ever want to say what *our* life is like, or that maybe *we're* the ones who stand to get hurt by this whole thing. Jesus Christ. It's like sending a bunch of guys to the moon, and everyone's sitting around wondering whether the *moon* is going to be all right. There isn't any way you're going to injure suburban people or suburban schools by busing in a few token black people. There's just no way. Anybody thinks that is just somebody who hates black folks no matter where they are: Africa, the south, the north, anywhere!" Sam was shaking his head in agreement. I thought Ronnie might cry. "Sam will tell you," he went on. "METCO's going to help me and everyone else in this bus. Maybe we would have ended up with the same sort of life if we'd stayed in Dorchester or Roxbury, but there isn't anyone who can know that. If this country can't find the place for what, how many are in here today, Sam?"

"Forty-five and two absent," Sam shouted back at him.

"Forty-five. Okay. If they can't find a place for forty-five, for forty-five thousand, then they better close up their doors, 'cause they've failed, not me, man. *They've* failed. You dig?"

"Right on, Ronald." "Right on, 'Woods,' " came the voices of students alongside him. Ronnie Harmwood slouched on the bench, his body jostled by the movements of the bus, his face immobile. Several students looked at me as if to say, Let's hear you argue that!

"I dig," I said quietly.

"All right," he said.

"You better get his words down, Tom," Sam suggested. "You'll never hear the case said better. No lawyer's going to outtalk that young man."

"I'll remember," I assured him. "Thanks for your time, Ronnie."

"All right. You talk to the others, you'll see what they got to say. Don't you go only by what I say. Everyone's got his own message. You got forty-five people in here, you should spend the time talking to each one. Then after that you go find the two who are missing."

"I'm going to try," I answered, but his advice was not the only thing on my mind. What continues to touch me is the way that those people who are obliged to be the "objects" of major social change, and busing clearly is just that, must be the very people who provide the perspective from which the rest of us make our assessments. Here were young people, no more courageous perhaps than many their own age, going through an experience which those of us who observe them were making larger than life. Suddenly they were soldiers, members of a children's crusade, freedom fighters, pioneers. We wanted any one of them who seemed especially outspoken or aggressive to speak for all the others, all the black students across the country in Michigan, California, Mississippi, Georgia, and Massachusetts. What is it that you people are going through now in this country? is what Ronnie heard in my questions. And still, it is not romanticizing him or rendering him larger than life to observe that this man had the integrity to say: I speak only for myself and for no one else. I am no bigger than what you see, no wiser than what you hear.

None of the three of us, moreover, not Sam, not Ronnie, not I, can speak freely anymore; we know what people are listening for. We have, in public, become the very politicians we openly chastise for their hypocritical ways and unhelpful diplomatic utterances. And yet this fifteen-year-old man, knowing full well that whenever one black student confesses to tension or unhappiness or the mildest case of classroom boredom the confession becomes political ammunition against the METCO program, against the golden opportunity, resists speaking for even one other person.

Another young person, Katherine Taylor Wyler, who is white, has spoken to me about busing. Once in her life Kit Wyler visited several neighborhoods in Roxbury. She is not certain whether she has ever been in Dorchester, or where for that matter Boston ends and Dorchester begins. She was in grammar school when her suburb voted an acceptance of the busing program. It meant nothing to her then; it means more now, especially right now, this week, following the publication of a report by a Harvard social scientist that tends to disparage the METCO busing program. She has English class with Ronald Harmwood, someone she does not call a close friend as she would others who are bused to her school.

"I size it up this way," Kit said one afternoon as we walked around the lush grounds of the high school. "I say that the busing program is a success despite the racist stuff that surrounds every move every black person makes in this community. The school is white, the majority of people are white, white people vote yes or no on the program, and then white people decide how many nonwhites can come to school here. Then, white people like you try to do studies on these black students and come out with your proposals. I know people who are supposedly evaluating what's going on in our Social Studies course who have never even been in the homes of one black family. But they have the right to say anything they want. And another thing, they think that black kids tell them the truth all the time. Like they're being open with them. It's ridiculous. Anybody can see that. So anyway, here you have all these black kids waiting for all these white people to tell them what's going to be happening to them. I don't think it's fair. I know I couldn't study all the time if people were looking at me every day as if I were about to do something bad, like commit a crime maybe. That's not right. I don't mean that black kids are criminals. I mean everybody's looking at them as though they were."

"I know what you mean, Kit," I interjected.

"Well, maybe you do, but a lot of people don't. And they're more important like, because they're here every day. I think they should just let these kids go to school and leave them alone. Why do they have to study anybody? They never studied the white kids in my classes who were flunking. They just let them go, so why do they have to look so hard at the black kids? They're not doing any worse. And what if they are? Suppose they were doing worse in their subjects than we are. What of it? It doesn't mean anything. It just means we've had an advantage over them since we were kids. That's all."

There were constraints on Kit and me too during our discussions of busing. I admit to imagining questions like: Do you date black guys, and do you see them after school, and are any of your best friends . . . ? With Kit, I found myself looking so closely at the busing issue that I actually could not see it at all anymore. It was like staring intently at an object and having it disappear, actually dissolve before your eyes. The whole busing issue is a ghost, I decided capriciously one evening returning home from an inner-city school. It's not really there, or at least that's not what it is. But in the news that night there was a story of a township having voted to reject METCO, and hence prohibit fifty black students from filtering in among fifteen hundred whites. So it was not a ghost at all.

"Of course it affects us," Kit explained with the patience of a gentle teacher. "What do you expect me to say? That I don't notice that they're here? Of course I see them. I see one boy and I say to myself, he's black. And I see another boy and I say to myself, there's Ted. And if you want to know would I date them, the answer is no. I wouldn't date *them!*" She said the word derisively, but it was clear that she was referring to individuals and resisting reference to a group. "I would date black men. If I liked them. And I have. And I have dated them. And that's all you or anyone else has to know on that subject. I'll write my own report."

"I'll not pry another inch," I promised her.

"That's good. I wish you'd tell my mother and father not to anymore either."

"I'm afraid that's not my business," I grinned at her. "Maybe it should be."

"Yes, I know." She sounded so wistful. "I wish it were though. I really wish it were. I think it would be much more valuable than to keep going around asking students about METCO. I think you should talk to parents, but don't ask them what they think. Retrain them to think like we do."

"We?" I wondered.

"We. The kids who are dedicated to make this thing work." It touched me that she would say it that way. So often one hears young people correcting themselves upon hearing what they fear is a platitude or cliché. Or perhaps they hear themselves as they imagine we might hear them. A young woman told me recently, "There's this Negro boy in my class who keeps wising off to the teacher. He keeps telling her that he can't hear what she's talking about, or he'll make so much noise most of the rest of us can't hear her. I don't think it's right. But I don't think he . . . I mean, I don't want this to sound bigoted or prejudiced, but I'm afraid to tell him to shut up because he might get his gang, you know, on me. But I'm going to tell him, gang and all, one of these days."

I waited for Kit to perhaps soften her words, make them less Apple Pie America: "dedicated to make this thing work." She never did. "If they'd leave us alone, we could work it out." She started moving rhythmically, clicking her fingers and bobbing her head. She was singing: "We can work it out . . . We can work it out." She stopped abruptly and blew out a long breath. "Amen!"

"That's why I say a man's a fool to try to say something honest about this busing business." Sam Tavorsky returned to his earlier statement. "You got parents and school boards, money, governors, mayors, people running for President, everybody, everything's in on this one. This is black against white. There's no room for nothing else. They got this fire started now over race, ain't anyone I know about to put it out. I'll tell you. You take the elections. You got to look twice at a man who'll send his kids to a public school. It's like they say, black against white, everybody else is going to have to stand aside. You don't need no Ku Klux Klan when you got people fighting against these kids I drive here. I'll tell you something else. I'm beginning to feel they're my own. I'm getting to care for 'em. You better watch out there, young fellow," Sam winked at me as he turned off Massachusetts Route 128 onto Route 9 East. "When that revolution they're always talking about comes, I'm going to be mighty tempted to be on their side. It's black against white.

No other way to be, and if you don't think that's a whole pailful of truth, then you sit down next to that Gloria Pei, third row, aisle seat. Little Chinese girl there. You talk to her, you'll see what I mean."

Gloria Pei and I were already friends. I had spent time speaking with her and her family when busing became a reality. Her mother was excited by the idea, but her father stood opposed to it. "They're missing the point," he had said. "They don't seem to realize that we don't identify ourselves as nonwhite. We are Chinese-Americans. Americans if you prefer. Not nonwhite. I don't want my children being bused if it means that the country can get away dividing its people between white and nonwhite. It makes us all sound like we're not quite proper people. This is a very important matter to us, Mr. Cottle, and I would hope you could take this message back to those who work with you in the universities. We are a different race. That is true. I am not like you, but I am also not a Negro. I am not superior to the Negro, nor am I inferior to the white. I am simply different. No better, no worse. But when I am placed in the category of nonwhite, I am being called inferior. I am being watched and segregated. My child is to be bused, then studied, then compared to the white child, but not to the black child. In the case of the Chinese, don't you see, Gloria, if we allow her to be a part of this program, is being doubly deprived of her cultural rights. This is all I am saying."

It was later decided that Gloria Pei would enter the METCO program in order to "improve her educational opportunities." No doubt it has meant a change in her life, disruptions and sadness, an elevation of spirit too. Like roots, her father's words have grown in her own personality and definition of herself. Busing has its political implications for her, just as it has its curious cultural payload.

"It is my chance now," she told me on the bus. "What I do with it is my own fault. My father is right. I didn't want to hear him that first time at my house, do you remember?"

"Yes indeed I do."

"Do you remember what he said?"

"Yes. I thought he was very strong and very eloquent."

"I didn't. I thought he was just standing in my way. I thought my mother was right. But *he* is. Well, they both are. She's right to want me to get the best education I can. But he's right to not let me ever forget what I am and where I come from. I don't blame METCO. It's not their fault. It's not even the suburbs' fault. It's all of us. You, me, all of us. Except for Sam." I saw her smile.

"You like Sam don't you?" Sam Tavorsky guided our bus through afternoon traffic.

"We all love Sam. He's a sweetie. I wish everyone could know Sam."

"I'm envious, I think."

"Of Sam?"

"Yeah, sure."

"He's a good person to envy. He takes each one of us as individuals. We aren't just kids to him. We're people. Everyone different, unique. That's the important thing. It's especially hard for the Oriental students. Spanish-speaking too. We have to be with the black students. Which is all right, don't get me wrong. But, you know, every once in a while I wish that I could either just be Gloria Pei or a member of the Chinese-American group. It's foolish, I guess, to believe that will ever be, but still . . . Well, for the moment I'm nonwhite, and I don't think that's going to change. Anyway, the way things are going now I'd just as soon be with the black students. I have lots of friends at school who are white and they understand why I prefer it the way it is. They're important in this whole thing too."

"White students?"

"Hmm. They get lost, I think. They don't always know what to say. Some are just bigots. I don't even know whether they know it, but they are. But lots aren't. They're really trying too. Between their parents and the administration, they don't have it so easy themselves. But I think of them as part of METCO too. They're a part," she concluded, "just like we are. Sometimes I even think I feel more sorry for them than I do for us." Gloria looked at me thoughfully, then shook her head. "No I don't. I don't feel sorry for them. Maybe I do. Oh, I don't know. Maybe . . . I feel sorry for *you*."

"For *me*? Why me?" For the moment I found myself outside the populations about which she was speaking. Her words suddenly made me a part of the issue, a part of busing, and I felt a chill.

"Because you look so hot." Gloria laughed and fell against the back of the bench.

"You're a nut," I responded. "Hey, thanks, though, I'll be talking with you."

"As always," she muttered, still grinning.

"As always," I repeated. "But maybe not when it's so hot. I'll wait for it to cool off."

"That's going to be a long time, Tom. If you're still talking about busing, it isn't going to cool off for a long time. You get my meaning?"

"Very well."

"As long as it's whites versus nonwhites, it's never really going to be cool."

"Fair and mild," someone yelled out behind her. He had been listening to our conversation, his hand holding the bar on the back of the bench, "but never cool, baby."

"Oh quiet, you," Gloria reprimanded him good-naturedly. She smiled at me as if to make certain I caught the humor of it; then she swung around in her seat and slapped his hand. He withdrew it quickly.

"Fair and mild, baby, but never cool," he repeated. "And storm clouds comin' *strong* on the horizon."

the integration of harry benjamin

self-conception, competence, and the conflict of communities

One of the students I met when riding the school buses from Boston's inner city to the suburbs was fourteen-year-old Harry Benjamin. Most of our conversations took place on the bus or around his home in the Roxbury district. On a few occasions, however, we found a moment — usually not much more than that — to speak together during school time.

The conversation in chapter seven occurred when Harry was sixteen. It took place one morning, quite literally, in the four minutes between his first and second class periods. What is clear from Harry's words are his intelligence, ingenuity, and sensitive appreciation of what school means to him and to many of his classmates. He carries an anger about school as well as positive concerns for it. But now, after two years as one of the seventy black students working among some fifteen hundred white students in this suburban school, he has come to believe that he cannot meet the school's standards. The values of the community, moreover, cause him to disparage his own past and minimize his talents.

There can be no doubt that one's self-conception and sense of competence are affected by one's experiences in school and by one's associations with various community representatives. Though we believe self-conception and competence to be psychological terms, they have their roots in society, culture, and interpersonal relationships. Schools and communities, therefore, have the power to convince people whether they are worthy or not. And at times this is done so covertly that a student himself is not aware that he is being victimized rather than enlightened by differences in values.

Let no one invoke this one young man's life as evidence that busing is a failure. Rather, let this conversation serve as a reminder that schools and communities cannot always impose their own values on students, but must honor the values and attitudes that students bring to class. For values are a cornerstone of students' assessments of their past history, their present capacities, and future potential.

"My problem," Harry Benjamin was saying one morning after English class, "is that I just don't know what the hell I'm supposed to make of all this bullshit they're teaching me. Man, they go throwing some of this stuff around like it's supposed to mean something."

"What were they discussing in there?" I asked him as we marched down the halls of the opulent suburban high school. "Any books in particular?"

"Yeah," he snapped back. "Greek tragedy. Now what do I know or care about Greek tragedy, I ask you that? Man, I don't even know where Greece *is*. And that's another thing. Before they go to speaking about this play or that play, like *Oedipus Rex*, they show us this map of Greece and then they got one of the Roman Empire. I can't get it in my mind where these places are in the world. I ain't ever traveled nowhere. I'd like to maybe, though . . ." and he started to dream, "I'd like to go to Africa someday."

The halls between 9:14 and 9:20 were filled with students running, walking, whistling, moping their way to second period class. That feeling of school. Everyone knows it. It has anxiety and reactions to authority and giddiness and depression, all the world and all the feelings of the world tied up with it. When I think of that word *microcosm*, which some inevitably apply to the nature of schools, I have to wonder whether they mean a collection of feelings more than anything else. Surely no one would say society is like this, an easy extension of, and elaborated form of school. Harry interrupted my thoughts.

"You know, strange thing about this place, you know, you were asking me before?"

"Yes?"

"School's kind of like the whole world only in miniature."

"It *is*?" I questioned him, somewhat surprised.

"Sure. Look. This place is doing its best to teach us who we are. School stinks a lot of the time but that's the way life is. That's what my father always says to me. 'You got to learn the hard knocks there,' he says, 'cause you're going to find out there is no perfect smooth sailing anywhere.' He says that all the time. I don't want to conform, you know, be like all the rest of the kids, but you can't always start out and be different. That ain't the way to be. You got to learn to take orders and give orders."

"But you make it sound a bit like the army," I replied.

"Yeah, maybe I do." One could see him thinking about his own words. "But school ought to be a little like that. You got to do things you don't like."

"Even like Greek tragedy?"

"Yeah. Even that. You surprised to hear me say that?"

"Yeah. I am a little, truthfully."

"Well, don't be. See, here's the thing you can't dig, so I'm going to make you understand."

"I'm ready," I smiled at him.

"Seriously," he started. "I'm black. Right?"

"Right."

"Everybody knows that, right?"

"Right."

"Don't need to tell anybody, right?"

"Right."

"See," he began to giggle although his teeth were closed tightly, "you're getting all the answers right."

"You watch me, man," I blurted out unthinkingly, "I'm going to get straight A's."

"Well, that'll be good, too. 'Least one of us is passing."

"I'm sorry, Harry. Go on."

"Yeah. Yeah. Okay. See, I got to learn about what the white kids are learning, otherwise I'm always going to be behind them. I'm going to have to work harder at all of this stuff, no matter what happens. I don't dig it most of the time but I'm going to stick it out. Man, there's no one in this school hates it more than I do when some sonofabitch teacher, white or black. . . . That's another thing. Don't make no difference, you know. Some of them black teachers can be just as bad or worse on us black kids. Like, you know, I'd take Levy over Henkle any time. Boy, he's a mean motherfucker, that guy Henkle. He ain't been no friendly cat to me, whereas Levy, he's been a good friend, or you know, straight with me. A regular guy." We were heading down the main stairs of the building, caught in a trafficking of bodies and a swirl of language, conversations, pinching, smells of high school. Harry Benjamin was the single black person I could see in this entire swarm of persons. I was checking for this as he spoke his piece — but not he. He just kept poking and shoving his way downward, his words flying out for anyone to hear. It wasn't as though he had rehearsed his sentiments exactly; it was merely that nothing he was saying was meant for me alone to hear.

"Okay. So that's the race part of it. Now, like I was saying, they got horrible cats teaching here. They boss us here, they boss us there; don't even give us a chance to listen to ourselves think and figure out what we are or who we'd like to be. But it ain't no matter. I'm going to take it so I can make it like all the families of these kids have made it. I don't want my children to have to be bused out to no white suburb someday. This shit's going to have to stop. Damn thing which near drives me crazy is how the white kids all think we're something so special or something. They really think we got something on 'em. They should only know." The crowd of white students was slamming up against us as our feet hunted first for one step and then the next one. We had reached the landing above the ground floor. I felt as if I were being carried along. Suddenly my anxiety about getting trampled to death, a highly unlikely fate, was supplanted by a more intense anxiety connected with the thought that this tide of adolescents might inadvertently sweep me into some classroom from which I would not be able to escape before making an utter fool of myself. And still, as we began the last descent from the landing, I saw no other black faces in the crowd.

"Part I don't like about this school I guess more than any other is how they keep looking at you and pushing you. It's like they got to always control us, keep us under wraps or something." For the first time he looked about at the swarm of noisy students making their way toward the various first floor classrooms. "Now you dig this scene?"

"Man, I've been jostled around in it seems like days," I said.

"Yeah, it's a sonofabitch, ain't it?"

"Yup," I said. He laughed.

"Well," he went on, "who's going to make trouble in a setup like this with all these people staring at you all the time. Ain't no place to even move an inch, much less get out of line. Man. You hear what I'm saying? Get out of line. They got me talking their way now."

In response I mentioned a mutual friend: "Matthew says that school pressures him like I pressure him. The phrase he used which I like is that I give him no corners to hide in and no windows to jump out of."

"I can dig it. I can dig it." Harry nodded assent and pleasure. "Someday there's going to be one great revolution. All the kids of this country are going to slug the shit out of their teachers. Oooeee that's going to be one beautiful day for us. You know, at one designated time all the clocks in all the schools going to hit their chimes and very slowly, very slowly mind you, all these cats going to get out of their little chairs and walk up to the front of the classrooms and SUE-WANG, they're going to knock their teachers right through the blackboards. I can dig it. I can dig it."

"That means some of the good teachers that you like are going to go under with the bad ones, right?" Always my fears about a revolution come back to me.

"That's it. Sorry about that, man, but that's the way it's got to be in times of revolution." He was smiling broadly. "SUE-WANG and they'll drop like flies. Got to do something about this overpopulation problem we got here in these halls. You just said it yourself. Too many goddamn people here. So we'll start first with the teachers, then, maybe if everything all goes according to plan, we'll knock out the administrators too. Then we'll really be running the show."

"You know," I started timidly, "it almost sounds like you've done a lot of thinking about this already."

"You better believe I have. I think about it every day in class." He laughed. "Every day I'm sitting in this class or that class rackin' my poor mind as to how to get school to be more the way I want it. Now you take 'math' here. I got math coming up, right?"

"You'll think about this vision in math too, eh?"

"Sure. Got to, man. Got to. Can't let the dream die, not now before we've gotten something under way. You'll see. Well, you won't see, but I'll be in there and Oates will be cranking on 'bout math and I'll turn on my revolutionary dream."

"Your what?" I hadn't heard his words properly.

"My revolutionary dream, man. My revolutionary dream." I *had* heard his words properly. "I'll be sitting in there figuring out just how we got to organize the entire country and get all the kids involved so that they can take over every school. I mean every school, man. Not just these suburban deals. All of 'em. In every state as well as Alaska and Hawaii. Even the school where you once went."

"Five hundred years ago," I muttered, trying to get him to have a little tolerance for an old man should a revolution come. He wouldn't have any of it.

"C'mon, man," he came back, looking at me as we neared the math class. Only a few minutes to go before that screeching bell would ring; then there would be silence. "You know what? You got a thing about age. You know that? You ain't so old that you can't remember school and your desires to explode it, or take it over. Or were you one of those nice little well-behaved dudes?" As he said these words two thoughts struck me, almost as arrows might. First, I had had a vision of blowing up a chemistry lab when I was a high school junior. A group of boys had gotten together to laugh over the teacher's absent-mindedness and misperceptions of the perfectly obvious. There was a time, for example, when we thought we would take the laboratory door off its hinges and get everybody inside and then put the door back before the teacher came in for class. This procedure would be necessary because the door was always locked. What kept us from doing it, we reasoned and probably rightly so, was that the teacher would never have noticed that we had gotten in without his opening the door for us. So, later on we thought of total annihilation. I remember the anxiety I had felt then as we spoke of, well, revolution.

The second thought was how much Harry Benjamin had changed as we had moved from the last seconds of first period English to the minutes just before second period mathematics. His resolute way, his willingness to adapt to a trying situation whose payoff in thirty years was as real to him now as the kids who milled in the halls, his conformity, were all being altered. His language, too, and the rules he might have resented, having to do with the game that ultimately constituted his schooling, had undergone tremendous transformations in these few minutes. The fact was he even seemed more handsome now than he did five minutes before, and if this were only my imagination, then surely he had grown several inches in this time.

"What you thinkin' about?" he asked me.

"About students and schools," I answered him. "Basically what you were saying."

"Yeah. Well, don't take it all too seriously, man."

"Well, I do, I suppose."

"You don't have to. It's only a dream, my stuff. I ain't about to get into any trouble here. If I did my father would draw the belt on me. I'd have to run away from here rather than face that."

"Well, that may be true," I said, "but you know, school must be terrible if all you're doing is sitting in class thinking about ways to overthrow it."

"School sucks!" Harry Benjamin looked at me, straight on. Now, at last, I believed him to be as close to what he really would be that one day. "It sucks! Ain't no one going to give you any argument there. Very few kids dig it. Every once in a while something good might happen. Might be in class or outside of class. But man, when you got to take it this way, day in, day out, you got to be mighty strong or mighty dumb not to be defeated by it. That's kind of why I plot to take it over. 'Cause I ain't so strong and I ain't so dumb either."

"That's about the way I felt when I went to school, Harry, 'years and beers ago.'" He smiled when he heard me use his father's expression. "I never thought I was dumb, but I also didn't seem to have the strength to do it the way it was supposed to have been done." He was deeply interested in what I was divulging. But it had taken his wild, melodramatic fantasy to get me to dredge up my meager little leftover feelings about school, feelings which come back to me like an old girlfriend's name the moment I step on school grounds, any school grounds, anywhere.

"You know what, dad?" he was about to enter the mathematics classroom. "This has been a groove. You're one of the few people that has leveled with me about this school jazz." But I haven't, I thought. I haven't leveled with you at all, Harry Benjamin. I'm giving you rehearsed, well-baked bits of my childhood that I don't mind parting with at all to anyone. I've got millions more like them. Don't you know that they don't mean a thing? "Yup," he was saying, "you're an honest dude, so I'll give you an honest ticket back. In return, like."

"I'd like to hear it," I said, shaking off what I believed to be the commencement of a line of unrehearsed portions, the parade of the raw bits of my history that I give only rarely, and even then reluctantly, and never, never once gave to any teacher that I can think of.

"My dreams about overthrow are extremist and all that. No one needs to tell me that." He switched his books to his left hand in preparation for opening the door with his right. For the first time he looked about warily, making certain that no one else would hear him. Then he waited for a girl to go into the room. "Hi, Harry," she said softly, the two words brimming with feeling.

"Hey, what d'you say, mamma." Then he looked at the mustard-color linoleum floor and began.

"I'm scared, man. I'm scared shitless in this place. Almost two years now I been coming here and I still get the 'flies in my stomach every day. Every morning before we leave. Every day. I don't belong here, man. Not just 'cause I'm black and everyone's white. It's just that it's all over my head. They got lots of teachers here telling me my talents are fine and I'm, you know, going to be all right. But they're jerkin' me off. It's going to be one helluva cold day in hell 'fore I get to making it here like you're supposed to. The thing is, no matter how hard I try it ain't never enough. I work harder than any of 'em and I can't do it. I just can't do it. I just can't do it, and I . . . I . . . I don't know who to talk to 'cause it just ain't easy to tell someone you're failing and you know they're keeping you practically no matter what 'cause you're black or you're poor or your father's an alcoholic or your mother's a whore."

The class bell blared in the hall and everywhere around me I heard doors slam. Quickly the noise diminished. A few stragglers dashed about along with those who were free this one period. "They're doing the best they can. So am I. I'm doing the best I can but it just ain't working out and *you* can't say a thing or figure out anything to do neither, 'cause you know it's true. Every last word I say."

And just like that he was gone.

chapter eight

schools
and
the
movie
of
the
mind

*politics, crime, and drugs—
a view from the other side*

as no one person ever serves as a perfect model or representative of other persons, so too no institution ever represents all institutions of its kind. Accordingly, when one's interest lies in education, it is essential that one travel to various cities and towns and speak to the people there. Regional differences and rural-urban distinctions are a vital part of education. And, although the temptation to compare schools, students, or teachers is often unremitting, trips to various schools at least widen our perspectives and inhibit us from speaking too authoritatively about education.

One of my trips took me to central Illinois where I met a young man attending a small rural school. Often our conversations took place walking between his house and school, and focused on the conflict he was experiencing between leaving home, essentially because of political differences with his family, and staying to work the land with his father. In Wally Brown's case, international politics along with an emerging history with his family has affected his education and choice of career.

On a trip to Pennsylvania, I met two young men enrolled in a large urban technical high school. Bobby Richmond and Phil Fannion had their own conflicts about families, education, and career, as well as their own day-by-day involvements with their school and community. Working the land on a tractor could not be a more foreign notion for these two young men, although they would share with Wally Brown the need for personal and economic survival and the hope that school could help them in this need.

In an Eastern city, I pursued the story of a young man in the city's black ghetto who, not unlike these other young men, fought a battle for survival, this one against drugs. In Samuel Williams' story, however, the battle was not against what one normally thinks of as drug abuse.

No doubt proper classroom behavior and obedience remain dominant ideals in almost all schools. Students learn laws and the price of breaking them. But schools, in addition, are affected by the laws and crimes of the society. In a sense, the conversations of chapter eight are united by this theme of education, laws, and crime. There are many forms of criminal action, and each one leaves its impressions on school and on the destinies of teachers, students, and administrators. Once schools may have believed themselves to be isolated from their communities and country, and, coincidentally, our stereotypes about school went unchallenged. But all of this has now changed. If schools are not directly influenced by the actions of a society, then they are at least implicated in them, and hence our earlier stereotypes must be buried.

I must confess that for a while what I was reading about high schools, grade schools, even colleges, was beginning to convince me. When the inventories, attitude scales, and reports compiled by the "sensitive" people and critics — "romantics," many have been called — were tallied up, I was in fact getting a rather consistent picture of American schools.

I could almost imagine the stereotypic pupil, teacher, and principal. Even their names seemed to fit them in some crazy way and contributed to the downgrading and saddening hurt many educators were discovering. There were powerful words, too, that some had fetched to describe the scenes and scenery of schools: words like *crisis* and *murder* and *rape of the mind*. America *was* in fact going under. It was true. An angry earthquake had rippled an enormous country, and the young, particularly those well ensconced in the little chairs bolted with iron to lift-top desks, would be the first to fall into the pits of a sunken dream. Some children have now been totally abandoned, the echoes of their voices long ago silent.

There is much being said and written about youth and education. Schools, or some of them anyway, have become garish marketplaces, with people swarming about them, gazing at the colors, at the spectacle and process of it all, inspecting the goods, the ideas, the children, the teachers too; and everyone assesses the facilities, seen and unseen. Feelings are being inspected more these days; intelligent people are intruding into the booths of education, often making schools more humane, often, ironically, making them even more constricting, self-conscious, and clumsy.

There comes a point when one must see it for oneself, or at least touch the boys and girls, the men and women who attend these schools. Despite one's biases and methods, limited or glorious, there comes a time when, as they say, seeing is believing. But this, I suppose, is the point: The images of school had been drawn so sharply for me, the marketplace and prison imagery delineated with such a vehemence and ferocity, that I had actually acquiesced to others' descriptions. It was like "seeing the news." I had come to believe that what I was perceiving was actually what the young people attending schools were experiencing. Indeed the portraits of students and teachers were so vivid and unequivocal that it seemed preposterous that anyone could utter such words as, "Well, my school's not exactly like this," or, "You should come to school with *me*, 'cause there's no book that could possibly describe *my* life."

But there was something else, something beyond mere accuracies and inaccuracies in description. Partly it was that I felt myself swept up in the myths and moods of America's myriad cultures. Somehow, and maybe

this is foolish to say, the poverty, the inhuman scenes and life founda-
tions dominating big cities were leaking into, of all places, the suburbs.
"Oppression" and words like it — another one is "dehumanization" —
were being heard in schools that advertised facilities the ghetto dwellers
I know would swoon over: like two swimming pools, or a men's gymnasium and a women's gymnasium, or university-approved science
laboratories more inviting than many living rooms I had visited. It
seemed that young people everywhere were crying oppression or mask-
ing the pains of education. Constraint, iron laws of regulation, hall
guards, and cabined spirits had become the catchwords of schools, the
ragged banners of educational communities, and, even worse, the stuff
of human experience. One could almost hear the cries of America's
children; no longer the war whoops of playground excitement and
physical adventure; no longer the deep, sustained breathing of timeless
concentration and self-propelled commitment; just the cries and danger
calls of a culture "caving in on itself," as a fifteen-year-old boy from the
Far West had said.

What then, was that single voice the critics, journalists, and educators had brought back to us from "the field"? The data of systematic
studies and the visions of people who look forward, free of artifactual
aids but limited all the same by their passions, seemed to be converging
on the same ground: "America's schools are failing," is what they said
again and again. "Schools aren't doing the job," is what they said. "They
suck," is what a young man told me riding the Boston subway to Ken-
dall Square. "They suck, man. You can't get educated in this country
without being crippled or maimed." A psychoanalyst had said much the
same thing when he wondered aloud whether "it is possible anymore
to be educated and still maintain one's dignity." He didn't even ask it
in the form of a question. It was as though he comprehended the implications of his words and had already resigned himself to the destruction
caused by that rippling in the earth now reaching "upward" to colleges
and "downward," for sure, to the most precious and yet still unformed
preschool nurseries, day care centers, and educational television experiments.

Still, I needed to see and hear for myself what cinematographers dis-
close. I needed a movie in my mind — of schools and of the one single
resource remaining, the one single resource worth preserving. How trite

it is sometimes to say "preserving human life." It's sentimental and dreamy, not sufficiently scientific. But when the windows of a school in a suburb are smashed at night as soon as they are repaired, the issue becomes one of human lives so bitterly defiant, so caked with adolescent fury, it seems almost comical that our attentions would rush to windows or the inability of chicken wire to protect them. Granted, broken windows make underpaid employees work that much harder in dangerous and degrading travail. And broken windows cause schoolchildren to shiver in their "homerooms." But the bullies also feel a chill — the angry, lonesome ones outside in the night, standing around, their bodies revealing tension, boredom, looseness, fright, sexuality, then angry boredom all over again. For they too respond to demands made upon them by an unseen sociology — their families perhaps, the loss of family perhaps — a sociology that drives them to engage in dangerous and degrading work. They too have felt a "calling," a military order that, when decoded, states: Destroy the objects, the symbols, the edifice, school! The only resource worth speaking about is human lives, all the lives that constitute school, or at least those lives one is able to know slightly through observation and brief friendship.

Samuel Jackson Williams is the sixth child of Clarence and Ernestine Williams. His family lives in a large black community on the second floor of a four-story walk-up. A man residing 850 miles away owns the building in which they live. They have never met him; he has never come to inspect this building nor, presumably, does he wonder about the eight persons who wait out the freezing cold nights in what is registered as "three and a half rooms, heated." A plasterboard partition, now with several holes in it, was erected in the middle of what used to be the living room. Two large mattresses lie on the floor on either side of the partition. The Williams boys sleep on one side, the girls on the other. "Three and three; it works out perfectly," I was told by their mother.

Sam is a short, slender boy. The kids around Feldsor Street call him "Wind," probably because George, his oldest brother, always said, "Sam is so little that if a wind ever comes up he's going to blow away and none of us will be able to find him." But although he's physically slight, one would never know it by his actions, for the tumult this one marvelous young man can kick up, especially at school, is breathtaking. "That boy will be the death of me," his mother always says with sighs of exasperation preceding a glowing pride. His parents love him intensely, but still they wonder how he is ever going to control that energy, particularly so that he might stay out of trouble in school and "in the streets with the other boys his age around here." Sitting in the back of the class, in mathematics say, this five-foot-six-inch young man "can cause more mischief than a pack of wolves," one of his teachers would remark in the school's cafeteria. "We just can't cool him off." And so they couldn't. Nor were they able to, until just recently.

Let us speak briefly about the experience of school. What it's like walking the six blocks to the neighborhood school yard each morning, picking up buddies, fellow pirates on the way, and feeling the fright of not knowing what the day will bring because everything — the people, the language, the very purpose of knowledge — seems so foreign and utterly unconnected to "practically anything that could make sense to anyone." Then there is the banter in the halls, resuming yesterday's conversations, a fight with Mollie, joking of course with "Machie," tweaking Jennifer Paulie's elbow, something that started in "bio" class where Sam discovered that when he pinched his elbow he felt nothing. For a few minutes he had been enraptured not by the structure of nerves but by the fact that here was a part of one's body, that is, a part of someone else's body that had no nerves, no nerves at all. "Hey, Jennifer, woman. Come here, baby, I want you to dig something over here."

To tone down this "hyped-up" youth, this "demon on wheels" as his dad called him once, to tone him down one Wednesday afternoon toward the beginning of winter, a teacher, after consultation with a physician in a handsome office, gave the boy a pill to swallow. He was told it was a vitamin, but it made him groggy and vomitous. Arriving after school at the little "clubroom" in the basement of the warehouse behind the church on Cleary Avenue, Sam went unnoticed for a minute or two. I saw him stagger a bit on the stair but I was not concerned about it. Sam's irrepressible imagination, I mused. A herd of low-flying buffalo must have flattened him when he ran and ducked from them on the school yard. Or maybe the Mafia finally caught up to this numbers-running hoodlum, who I am certain carried more bets and favors in an hour than all of Western Union in that section of the city.

Then, suddenly, he fell over, face forward, cracking his jaw and the left side of his chin on the arm of a chair. We ran to him. "Sam. Sam. What is it, man?" "C'mon, 'Wind,' open those screwy eyes of yours. C'mon, boy!" "Jesus, Tom, he's dead!" one of the boys cried. Another screamed "Help!" so loudly the plea should have awakened the entire city, if not all its gods. Sam was comatose, his eyeballs rolled upward. I remember thinking as we lifted him into my car, which would not start at once because a few of the guys, as a joke, had messed with some of the battery cables ("Really cute, you guys," I had said, "really very, very cute."), that these constitute the times I yearn to be a doctor, a savior maybe, but surely someone able to offer competent medical attention. But then, should not schools provide medical knowledge? Sex education certainly, and car mechanic training for boys and girls. But what good is "trig" or Latin or anything if your buddy breaks a leg, or drives a nail through his cheek, or falls flat, comatose with a broken face in the clubroom where you were about to start some after-school nonsense which had as its purpose nothing more than communion and simple friendship?

The case was never resolved. This one experience of school, these first frames of film, showed a teacher administering a depressant drug to a child who "just acted up one too many times." Sam had been running around in the back of a study hall, flying planes or pinching girls or drawing dirty pictures. So, the teachers, having stood all they could, made a chain of telephone calls until finally a superintendent or principal or doctor or someone gave the green light. Truthfully, no one was quite certain just who gave the final approval. No one knew of the congenital liver disturbance from which Sam suffered.

Ernestine Williams had spent the day, like all other weekdays, at the weaving factory where she worked from eight until four. The factory's telephone number was listed in the official records of all three of her children who attended that one school. Often she had reminded the school to call her should there be an emergency involving any of her children. "I know I should be here waiting for them when they come home," she had said to me, "but if I don't help my man we just won't have enough. I've got to work, boy, I've got my work to do. God doesn't always give us the choice." The factory phone never rang. Everyone in the city, I think now, went about his work or play that one afternoon as the poison of a depressant drug spread through the bloodstream of a fifteen-year-old boy who, I had now come to believe, might very well blow away in a windstorm.

At the hospital, generous young residents and interns came to our rescue. Sam was in good hands. On his record, on a pink form clipped between silver metal covers, someone with illegible handwriting had written his name, age, the date, his home address, the school's name, both his parents' names, and beneath these, the one word OVERDOSE. "We've got to write that," a young medical student in wrinkled "whites" told me, his tired face showing strain and a peculiar sort of hopelessness. "He's the fifth case this year from that goddamn school. The kids ought to rip it down already. How can this happen? I just don't get it. I swear to God." We stared at each other as though, separately and then together, we were attempting to marry our professions and passions so that no one anywhere would ever have to suffer again. Then he turned and walked down the long corridor in the direction of where Sam lay. Resting on a cart-table and babbling, Sam was being aided by a lovely black nurse and a handsome white policeman whose right hand protected Sam's tragically dulled face.

The conversation that followed later that evening with Mrs. Williams ultimately led to no tangible settlement. Even as she wailed her desperation and grief, she herself knew nothing would happen. Nothing at all. Sam would be all right; in fact he would be home the next day. But what could she do? One does not transfer students to different schools just like that, or make political or legal trouble. "That takes money *and* power, son," she explained to Charles. Maybe it *was* "best to forget it and thank God Almighty that nothing worse had happened to Samuel," as her husband had been urging, his own hands trembling as he stood behind his seated wife, holding her by the shoulders.

Is it horrible to say that one almost cherishes these moments of tragedy and explosive fury? Is it unforgivable to admit that, with a sorrowful policeman there and with a family — a mother and father and five children — and the small homely rooms and the partition, the differences in sex and age, or race and preoccupying social status tend to disappear, as though the wind had blown them away, and people stand before one another concentrating on the destiny of schools and children, neighborhoods, and perhaps humanity as well?

There were more movie frames in a farm town south of Champaign, Illinois. In the hot spring months when the air is painfully dry, some of the young people walk to the schoolhouse there, barefoot, the rough edges of their overalls caked with dust and pollen, and their feet soot black from the melting tar of the roads. It is exactly what the media and our imaginations portray. Twenty-four students in the eleventh grade sitting together at worn-out desks that their parents were eager to replace but that the children demanded be retained. "They were about the only history we had," Walter A. Brown, Jr., told me. "They've got out-of-date books which they usually don't care about, but the real stuff of America is in this room. Look at those walls — and that ceiling. Bet you never saw real beams like *that* before. Knock those down and the whole damn place'd fall on your head. Guy wasn't kidding who made this place." Then, looking not unlike his dad, Walter A. Brown Sr., he said: "It'll outlive you and me both, put together."

I spent several days with Wally, the name his mother called him when her husband was not around, which was most of the time. We walked to and from school and back into the woods behind the "out barn" belonging to his neighbors, the Cleavers.

Five years ago, when he was eleven, Wally Brown began assembling his snake collection. He loved the small garden snakes and the few other varieties he was able to find here in a region where a man eighty years old had claimed that in all his years he'd "never seen but two or three snakes. I'll make it five," the old man said, smiling at me one Sunday at church, "since you were born in Chicago and got all kinds of romantic notions about us downstaters." Nonetheless, Wally was collecting snakes, giving names to most of them, like Hissy and Rodney, and learning from the high school science teacher, Harry Autrey, just what had to be done to preserve these specimens. "It was just like a laboratory here. A special secret laboratory that only Mr. Autrey and I knew about." Actually, Mr. Brown, Sr., had helped his son transport cabinets and a sturdy walnut work table to a small shack near the mouth of the cave where Wally was studying herpetology. He had made the table especially for his son's research.

It had been an exciting year, even though the hours of English and social studies seemed to have passed more slowly than before. Wally's discovery of science meant the end of pedestrian schoolwork and the commencement of wondrous hours of intensive study and technical adventure. To hear Wally's recollections was to be reminded of the majesty of learning. He worked on his snake collection every afternoon as fact upon fact piled up in the cave, and on the table as well. Quickly the chemistry of preservatives and treatment dyes of cells came to be simple childish puzzles easily solved. Moreover, he adored Mr. Autrey, who during their walks to the out barn, laid plans for a future of university study, crowded laboratories, biological field-training stations, libraries, and expeditions to all the world's continents to hunt for the most unusual of snakes and reptiles. "Everyone I met, I told them I was going to be a herpetologist. They'd always say, 'That's nice,' but I knew none of 'em even knew what I was talking about. Once I pulled a snake out of my pocket and shoved it in this lady's face outside of church. 'See, this is what I'm going to be when I grow up,' I said. My mother slapped me, but my father, he laughed out loud. It was really great. God, the things you can get away with as a kid in school."

But all of this was in the past. For there is not always a continuity of school years nor a logical correspondence between intellectual interests. Learning knows the most complicated of twistings and bendings. The snake collection is long since gone. Indeed, by now, Wally informed me, all the snakes are probably dead. As the winter of seventh grade began, those snakes that had been properly preserved were taken to the local animal museum where today a few are still exhibited, with Wally's name, in glass cases; but Wally has almost totally disassociated himself from them and strangely, too, from that entire part of his life. It is as if he has leapfrogged over a large clump of years. Some of the snakes, his special ones, were buried in a plot, the location of which he once vowed he would never reveal, although during the days I spent with him he laughingly recalled every secret of the snakes as though that part of his past had to be, finally, relinquished. More recently, the little cave has become a place where he can escape, drink beer with a friend, study American history, or "best of all, make love with Jeannie."

It is a special feeling, these high school juniors reported, going to this old schoolhouse with its few facilities, its "falling apart" library where smoking is prohibited but where no one seems to take notice of "a little hanky-panky" behind the few stacks of books. Eighteen miles west of here on the interstate highway, just beyond the Mt. Washington turn-off and sitting up on a little knoll, is the region's largest high school. Every March, that plush school and its fourteen hundred students nearly turn inside out over the possibility that their basketball team will make it to the state's Sweet Sixteen Tournament and earn the esteemed trip to the University of Illinois to meet the great ones from the north, south, and west — "the teams loaded with all those sneaky colored boys" — right on the floor where Havlicek, Mount, Jones, and Lucas once played. For they too were once in high school, aiming at college and the competition of the Big Ten. Could school be any more than that?

What makes the feeling special too, is that the young people in this little school want no part of that life, or of "city life" for that matter. Most of their fathers are farmers or associated somehow with the farm industry. Wally's dad has been growing corn and soybeans since he was a boy. He went to the same school as his son, did his lessons just to obey the wishes of his own parents, but knew "it would never really amount to anything, that is, the math and the English wouldn't. It was good for us, I suppose, but we finally had to quit and go to work. That's where we ultimately belonged." Now the school schedule is arranged so that during the cold season the students cram especially hard so that they can help their parents with the extra labor required during autumn and spring picking and planting. In biology they are learning about agriculture. Once every two weeks a man from Carbondale comes to speak to the boys about progress in farm machinery and agricultural chemistry. There is no questioning, no doubting during these sessions, for the land is life; the fields are, in their way, sacred, and weather is the demon or goddess that manipulates life and the daily routines of everyone in the community.

Still, the boys and girls of this generation, as their parents realize, are different. No one seems to know for sure "just where they're going to end up. It's kind of frightening," Mrs. Cleaver said one afternoon. "Strangest sight in the world is to see these kids with their long hair and their beards and those Indian bands around their heads working with their fathers out there. Some of the fathers are embarrassed as all get out to be seen with some of their sons. We ain't this way. And Walter, this young man's father, that is, isn't neither." I looked at Wally who gave me an affirmative look. "But I don't think we're going to be able to keep them here once they finish at the schoolhouse," Mrs. Cleaver was continuing. "They got it in their minds to go to college and I can't see them coming back here after that. Do you? You know this brand of kids. What do *you* think?"

"I guess I agree with you, Mrs. Cleaver. It's pretty clear now that a lot of kids are leaving home for good."

"Seems kind of sad, though," she went on, speaking almost to herself, or to her God. "Sure would be sad to see these farms go under and the land just die. That's what'll happen if no one works it, and you can't expect these men to go on forever. We all die sometime, that's for sure," she laughed slightly.

"Too true," Wally muttered, looking at me and fingering the little button he wore pinned to the flap on his shirt pocket. The button showed a glistening white dove on a baby-blue background. "Too true."

In many ways, the war was changing the young people and, with them, the face and substance of their school. The films of Indochina were seen here every night, as they were everywhere else, and just about everyone had known a family somewhere in the district who had lost a son. The Cleavers' neighbors on the north, Harold and Mollie Springer, had lost their second oldest boy less than a year ago. Their first child was born with cerebral palsy and so Billy, that is, Staff Sergeant William Arlo Springer, had carried more than a family name and a local reputation with him to war. He had carried health, masculinity, and the genes, probably, for a stable evolution. Now his parents, his one crippled brother, and his three younger sisters had become beneficiaries of a minuscule amount of money; and because the other William Springer, Billy's uncle, had died of pneumonia at twenty-three before fathering a male child, the Springers' line would end with the death of Harold Springer.

The young Vietnam veteran was buried in the small cemetery not too far from Wally's cave, behind the town's main streets on the eastern tract of land owned by the Methodist Church. The American flag that had accompanied the casket from Asia now hung in the school. For days after the burial, social studies and English classes had debated the inevitability of wars. Students read furiously, gathering together the makings for arguments. The senior boys were frightened; college applications were coming to be invested with whole new meanings. Suddenly, the school-house was inundated with copies of the *Chicago Tribune,* the *St. Louis*

Post Dispatch, The Nation, and *U.S. News and World Report.* History and government had come alive, ironically, on the heels of death. Less than a mile away in the flat, rich earth of southern Illinois lay a boy mutilated by a mine, which, someone had claimed, had been assembled in a factory not far away in Indiana. "Can you imagine that," Mrs. Cleaver had remarked. "That fine young man just lying there and his parents not even sure if it's really him."

"I don't understand," I said.

"Well, you know . . . Wally, you shouldn't be hearing this talk," she caught herself.

"Mrs. Cleaver, I'm not a *child,*" Wally responded smartly, standing up to a height I had never imagined he could attain. "I ain't running from this kind of stuff, but I'll be damned if I'm going to end up like he did."

"God forgive him," she said. "I don't know what they're teaching these kids in the schools anymore. I swear I don't. Burning the flag and all."

"Now wait a minute, Mrs. Cleaver," Wally shot back.

"Hold it. Hold it," I said laughingly. "I'm just a reporter here, you know, not a boxing referee. You're going to have to settle all this after I go."

"Well, she's making a lot of uncalled for . . ." Wally tried again.

"I know, I know," I interrupted. "Mrs. Cleaver, could you just finish that last thought of yours."

Her voice was quieter now. "Well, I was only going to say that there was a lot of talk that maybe the coffin was empty, 'cause the boy was so, you know, badly injured. You know how it is. There was some talk, that's all."

Eloise Cleaver had retired from teaching at the little schoolhouse three years before. She was "getting on in years," and the profession had changed since "her time." She felt, moreover, that a certain modicum of appreciation had not been shown to her, and, anyway, thirty consecutive years of service was enough to give to any one institution. Her own mother had attended the little schoolhouse and later had taught for a few years in the seventh and eighth grades, but "that was nothing like thirty consecutive years." A lovely dinner at Nordley's Steak House and a silver serving tray culminated her tenure with the school.

The air was still and dry. In this region of Illinois the land is almost perfectly flat and magnificent in its appearance of endlessness. The sky zooms upward from the horizon, and occasionally one imagines that in a matter of hours a man and woman could walk together right up to the horizon's edge and look down to the source from where the sky ascends. There is a glory in this central Midwest region in the scenes the students see from their schoolroom windows. There is an almost embarrassing purity here where life and death, and learning too, seem less complicated — not necessarily more simple, just more discrete and finely etched.

"There's no time to be a-wasting," Wally's mother must have said ten times in the few days I visited with the family. "Now go do your homework, Wally, so as you can help your father with the after-dinner chores." He always obeyed her, carrying volumes of a second course in algebra or an intermediate German text to his room. There he might just sit at his desk, watching the squirrels play in the branches of the huge oak tree on the front lawn, but he did obey her. Homework, dinner, the after-dinner chores, "two more days of crummy school and then the weekend," a ride to Tolono maybe, a trip to the Lake of the Woods with Jean, and more time to figure out just what to do about the gnawing political differences between himself and his father. School was right in the middle of it. College had become a necessity, but it would mean leaving home, and in a way that meant "letting Dad down."

"I read a lot about youth," Wally told me at the train station as we waited together for my train to the north to arrive. "What I like about a lot of the writers is that they give me a good feeling for young people around the country. You know, the kinds of kids I'll never meet on my own. But no one really ever comes to visit *our* town. We never even get visitors from the capitol in Springfield to see what's happening in school. Well, maybe all kids feel that way."

"How much does school matter to you, Wally?" I had asked. We sat side by side on the smooth, curved waiting-room bench.

"Oh, that's too tough," he responded, smiling. "It's always hard to say just what makes a difference. Of course, school is about all I do when I'm not working with Dad. And all the kids I know, just about, are the ones I go to school with. Like Jean." He turned and grinned at the young woman who sat silently on the other side of him. She had been particularly quiet that day. Wally had advised me, "She's ticked 'cause I told you her and I made love together. She couldn't believe anyone would talk about things like that to anyone, especially someone he hardly knew." Jean tried to manage a smile. "Come on," Wally urged, and gave her a love pat. "You been a bitch all day," he murmured quietly. "You know that?" She said nothing.

"Where were we? Oh yeah, school. Good old school. Yeah. Well, like, everything that's happening, practically, ties into school somehow. Like college and what I'm going to do, which I can't decide. And of course the arguments with dear old Dad. I understand his position, though. I can see why guys like him, given his background and all, would think we should be in Vietnam. But we're different. That's all it is. He knows it as well as I do. We just don't talk about it when we're doing work. There's no sense anybody getting hassled over it. He's got his theories and I got mine. And we respect each other and aren't really getting, you know, the other guy to change. He knows I love him. I'd do anything for the guy; he'd do the same for me. We don't have any secrets. Lots of things you don't have to talk about with your old man; they just know. It's too bad schools don't treat us like he does. You know, with respect. There'd be less trouble if they did."

Train departures always yield up movie scenarios. Many people, I am sure, have felt this. Wally and Jean waited until I was out of sight. We waved and waved. First them, then me, then Wally alone, then me again, then all three of us together, their visions blurred now by the distance and by the steam hissing out from the pipe nozzles beneath the cars. Soon the land was rolling by faster, faster, and with the even window frames on the opposite side of the coach's aisle this unsteady series of images, too, became movielike. Frame after frame of placid, monochromatic earth, and then a barn and silo would rush by, right to left, and then there would be the land by itself again. Still more frames of the land, empty of people and livestock, disguising the richness it would yield in a matter of weeks.

Two great young people I may never see again despite the promises to exchange letters, particularly when college application time would come up next autumn. It would be nice to see that boy and girl come East. Maybe, though, they'd like the far West — University of Washington maybe, or Stanford, or Santa Cruz. Kids out there should meet these kinds of kids. It's their gentleness that touches me. Maybe, though, I'd best leave them alone to fend for themselves. They hardly need my kind of educational colonialism. They have their work and their schools. And the land. Small amounts of land to be sure, but whatever else happens there are a couple of acres back there that Wally Brown, Jr., dug up, planted, and nourished all by himself, with a slight assist, naturally, from the God that he and his girl both believe in with all their strength and intellectual fervor.

"One thing's for sure," Wally had said following that tense meeting with Eloise Cleaver. "Only God knows who's in that box in the cemetery. Only God knows where Willie Springer really is. The rest of us are left to guess. And that, stranger from the East, they can't teach you about in any school. Not even at your Harvard." *My* Harvard, I had mused. Stranger from the East, indeed. And you, Wally, a child of the land.

In the middle of an eastern city, I was struck again by a movielike vision. Here it was the filtering of bodies in and out between the spindles of the iron gates surrounding Boys Technical High School. The buildings resembled a prison. "Don't look so good of course," an assistant principal had explained when he saw me inspecting them, "but let's face it, we leave this place open, unguarded, they'll take everything that's not nailed down and we're out of business like that!" He snapped his fingers. Still, it seems difficult to imagine that anything bad could ever erupt from the young men that attend classes here. To be sure, their swaggers and bragging and jiving reveal the tension they hold, but that does not imply that trouble logically would result. And yet, somewhere in these schools, in these thousands of American schools, lurk the teachers who hurt and the administrators who hurt and the students, too, who hurt; all of them, secret warriors laying claim to the authority, the power, and the "turf."

"I'll show you where it is," Andy Barnett said to me, referring to the auto mechanic shop. His voice was so low and his speech so tired and worn that I wondered whether he might be in the throes of some kind of drug trip. Eight boys had been expelled two weeks before my visit to the school, and Andy's gait and sullen stares were convincing me that either he was "strung out" or that the place, the ambience, the walls and floors and lighting, the way the doors swung open and closed, the paint colors, the texture of the building materials, the broken windows and faulty heating system, the dank basement shop rooms, the putrid smells in the locker areas and gymnasium, the stench of the latrines, the rusted fence and the ugly frozen grounds, everything, had finally tapped the very physiology of this one boy and the eighteen hundred other boys who attend this institution.

I'm telling you, I said to the unseen character who invariably appears when I visit schools like these, and prisons and mental hospitals and certain factories too, you'd have to pay me one helluva lot of money to attend this place. And as always, he would answer me, you aren't kidding, man. This place, buddy boy, you can have. Me, I got no fascination with poverty areas and mangy high schools. Give me suburban living with trees and grass and nice schools for children . . .

"Down this corridor at the end on the left," Andy was pointing for me.

"Thanks, Andy. I appreciate it. Maybe I can catch you later. I'd like to get your impressions of 'Tech' too, if I might."

"Huh? Yeah. Sure. I'll be here. No place else to go," he responded in his flat, dull way. I watched him walk down the corridor in the direction from which we had come. He seemed disconnected from time.

My two guys were in the "car shop." Funny, suburban students for me are young men and women; rural ones, boys and girls maybe. But here, in the technical school where the Poles, blacks, Italians, Lithuanians, and Germans send their sons, where everything you see is labeled like exhibits in an arboretum, "Inner-City Poor," everyone is a "guy." Funny, too, by emphasizing their ethnicity or race, factors that usually matter little to them, do I, in a sense, deny that they are wholly American? Is someone more American than they? Or more human, perhaps, and thereby deserving the title "young man" rather than "guy"?

The noise in the shop was excruciating. Lathes, metal drill press machines, table and band saws for woodworking, and hand drills at several workbenches were all running at the same time. The young men in the shop, even those standing two feet apart, yelled their messages at one another. Heads here and there nodded agreement. I overheard communications like, "I'll cut it three-eighths of an inch light, and if it doesn't fit we'll take a sliver more." On a wall near the entrance, coats and hats hung on colored enamel hooks. Leather and suede jackets with belted backs, and a few motorcycle studded ones as well, hunched side by side. Quite a change from the lockered corridors where, even with combination locks, everybody at one time or another has experienced a theft. Here, everything was in the open.

Twenty-three guys at two o'clock on a Thursday afternoon, working away, with the early spring day barely visible through the ceiling-high half windows.

"How's it going?" I yelled into Bobby Richmond's ear.

"Beautiful, man, if you dig radiator lattices."

"If I dig *what?*" I yelled back.

"What'd you say?" he yelled, his gorgeous smile reminding me that I had no business in the world being here with him and his colleagues.

"If I dig *what* I said?" I yelled louder. What a way to do research.

"Radiator lattices, man. *Grills* to you."

"Oh," I said, no better off.

"You ever look inside your car, Tom?" Phil Fannion screamed at me as Bobby hammered on a gray metal plate with a two-pound hammer and a large chisel.

"Of course. What do you think, I'm a city dude?" I came back, eager to reveal my ignorance.

"That's *exactly* what I think you are." Phil laughed and turned to Bobby to relay the interchange. Bobby's face exploded joy on hearing the punch line. He looked up at me, still leaning over his work, laughing and shaking his head from side to side. "What are we ever going to do with this city dude?" was written all over his face.

"Is it always this noisy in here?"

"No," Phil answered. "Sometimes it's so quiet in here the Philadelphia Boys Choir comes over to practice." He looked at me quizzically, then broke out in laughter. Again, the dialogue was relayed to Bobby who laughed, naturally, but failed to look at me as his concentration just then could not be broken.

Gorgeous movie shots in here. It was a marvelous feeling, better than I had known in a school for a long time. Men at work, all but two of them students, engaged in making real products that one could see taking shape. Many of the students were sweating. Sawdust cemented by perspiration caked the faces and thin stocking caps of those working on the lathes and table saws. In the area of the room where the mechanical equipment was bolted to the floor, everyone wore protective goggles, some tinted light orange to maximize light. One could feel the significance of the work by the way the goggles were raised and lowered. The two instructors were as absorbed in the various enterprises as any of their students. Wearing long, gray laboratory coats, they moved among the workbenches checking, inspecting, demanding changes or reformulations of design, and staring intently at blueprints or drafting sketches for clues to major hitches.

Nelson Thackery advised Bobby: "I'd place your rivets four inches apart, plus or minus an eighth. But you're going to have to watch the casing here and here 'cause the support brackets may not hold the force of the press later on."

"What about a metal shim to enclose the edges for more support?" Bobby had yelled above the noise.

"No go," was the authoritative response. "Do that and you have no opening for the lock cylinder and drain. Even if you could, you'd never get a two-inch bit inside the casing once the support was soldered."

It made sense to the student. A minute of technical talk and he and Phil had all the advice and encouragement to carry them through until the following week when the next stage of the radiator casing would be ready for assembly. No authority issue; merely consultation with a professional. Tangible problems yield tangible solutions and hence progress. The young men were silent again, speaking only with their fingers from time to time on the metal apparatus locked in a bench vise.

I had come to know these men only slightly, though considerably better than the others in the shop. Both were doing poorly in their academic courses. In mathematics a teacher was brutalizing the class, despairing over thirty-eight "pathetic mentalities" as he called them, and bemoaning his fate of having to teach them. In English, another teacher seemed to have forsaken literature and was spending the time "making politics" as Bobby referred to it. Discussions centered about the Panthers, union organizing, what high school students can do. Several times during the classes I observed, mention was made of the oppression of the working classes and the need to start a revolution "right here in these kinds of understaffed prisons called urban technical high schools."

"Usually, Pearson [Frederick Pearson, the English teacher] just tells us the only problem we face is just being black, but because you were here he didn't say it today," Phil explained to me. "Sometimes I don't mind all the political stuff, but sometimes it's one helluva drag. What the hell good is it this cat tellin' us we're black? If we don't know that, who does?"

"'Nother thing," Bobby went on, "is that Pearson and Mullahy and these other cats really don't like most of the guys 'round here."

"He's right," Phil nodded.

"You know, they used to have this stud Grimshaw, or somethin' like that. When you'd wise off in car shop he'd just whup you. Right in front of everyone."

"You ever see that?" I suppose I hoped they would fill out my imagination.

"No, but I heard from a guy —"

"Yeah, once," Phil interrupted his friend. "Clemie Treevin's older brother, I can't think of his name, but he was messing around right where we were at today. Old man Grimshaw threatened to chop his finger off on the band saw."

"You kiddin' me, man?" Bobby asked his friend.

"Would I shit you, man?" Phil came back at him. "Like I said, he's going 'round saying, 'I think I'll just take the tip off this guy's little pinkie.' Showin' everybody too. Man, you should've seen Treevin. He was petrified silly."

"I'm getting sick just hearing about this," I said.

"You and me both," said Bobby.

Phil smiled. "I ain't shittin' you, man. That's what he did. I saw it myself. Finally, he just gave him a couple whacks on his ass and told Treevin he'd throw him out of school if he ever did something like that again. Tom, you don't like the noise in the shop?" I nodded. "Well, you could hear a pin drop that day. We was all standin' around shittin' in our pants. But they got rid of that guy. One month he was fired. Bam, he was gone. Just like that. Only good thing they ever done 'round here."

"You like the new guys, Phil?"

"Yeah. They're all right. Give you trouble once in a while, but mostly, like, it's all right."

"Yeah, it's all right," Bobby concurred. "Could be worse, I s'pose."

"But you like the machine shop, don't you?"

"Sure."

"I mean, it's . . . school's good during those hours, isn't it?"

"Yeah, you ain't kiddin'. I wish all day I could just stay down there and do my work," Phil responded.

"I wish so too," I muttered.

"I thought you didn't like it down there, dude," Bobby offered smiling.

"Not for *me*. I mean for *you* guys. It would be nice if you guys could just do your work all the time when you like it that much."

"Yeah. That'd be a groove," Phil said. "But then it wouldn't be school, would it?"

"Say it, brother."

"Yeah. I guess you're right. It probably wouldn't be school. Funny. . . ."

"You know you're some kind of heavy cat for a honkie," Bobby grinned at me. "Some heavy cat."

"What d'you mean?"

"Well, you know, worryin' about us that way, and about the school. You never went to no school like this, did you? You probably never even spent that much time in a car shop before, right?"

"That's right."

"And you're worryin' about us."

"He ain't worryin', man. He's studyin' us. Ain't that right, man?"

"Yeah. I'm filming you."

"Yeah, so where's your camera supposed to be?"

"In my mind."

"I tell you, Phillie, this here's one helluva strange cat. You're a strange cat, Thomas, my boy." We all laughed then and pounded one another's shoulders and arms.

"You're pretty cute yourself," I dared.

"Hey now, careful, man. We ain't that close, 'sweetie boy,'" Phil defended.

"I *knew* it," Bobby was shaking his head. "I knew it."

"You going to be here tomorrow, Tom?" Phil was asking. Bobby had already started to walk away, his shoulder brushing up against the tall iron fence.

"I leave tonight. I've got to get home."

"Yeah, I figured." Overhearing us, Bobby suddenly returned.

"You going to come back?"

"I hope so, but I don't know when."

"Hey, we should exchange addresses. You got some paper?"

"Yeah. Here. Tom, you got a pencil?"

"Good."

"Where the hell's my ball-point pen?"

"Yeah. Here, you can write on this book."

"Where? Here all right?"

"Must have left it in my locker."

"Can you read my writing?"

"Sure, fine."

"No trouble."

"Great. Here. How's that?"

"Beautiful."

"Perfect. So . . . O.K."

How many times had this scene been portrayed? It was like a train station parting. All of the political anger, the racial differences, and age disparities vanished in the exchange of autographs and people connecting, even when they know that so much of what society is and stands for keeps them distanced, keeps their unborn children distanced as well. Always there is the exchange of addresses and the promise to let them see a manuscript should one get written. Always there are remarks like, "I'll protect you by disguising your identity," and their ingenuous insistence that they want no aliases but, instead, seek all the fame and notoriety an article might fetch. Then they walk back into the streets and I leave their city.

Bobby Richmond's father was killed in a car accident. He, his mother and four sisters now live in a housing project not far from the school. A year ago Yvonne, his oldest sister, was raped in the boys' locker room at her school by a man whose identity is still not known. Some insist it was a teacher; others say it was one of the school's policemen. Soon afterward she quit school. Another sister, Arlene, withdrew from high school in the tenth grade. Her pregnancy left no doubt in the minds of the school board members that she would have to quit school. What bothered her most of all was that some local social workers had urged her to have an abortion. "They couldn't understand why I wanted my baby more than all the schooling in the world." For three months she attended class in the high school adjoining the yard of Boys Technical High, and despite having to run to the lavatory two or three times a day to vomit, she kept her secret, the blessing as well as the anguish, as long as she could from every single person in the world. Finally, there was no more secret, and she left school and has not returned.

Phil Fannion never knew his father. Matthew Josiah Fannion, Jr., was dead, or had disappeared — Phil continues to doubt the veracity of the death story — by the time Phil was born, the youngest son of Matthew and Louise Parker Fannion. Both of his brothers had been active members in a neighborhood gang, one of them having been seriously knifed in the groin during a fight with a member of his own gang. Several times his mother almost died of renal failure; the last time, the pains were so severe her cries could be heard across the yard in the Richmonds' apartment. In the middle of the night, two policemen came and took her in an ambulance to the county hospital, the attendants there muttering things like, "If she makes it, it'll be a miracle." Phil did not miss one day of school. "I had no place else to go," he sighed. "I sure wasn't any good to anyone anywhere else."

Neither boy feels he has any business being in school. "It just keeps me from my job," Bobby had said. Both work; both will always work, but school means "seven hours wasted when eight, ten, fifteen bucks are waitin' to be earned." Car shop, however, is different. The boys adore their work. The clock is rarely watched and, strangely, nothing is ever stolen from the jackets which hang from the enamel hooks as easy prey. It's a man's world; men's machines, men's noises and effort and smells remain there. Most of the students prefer sports, obviously, but the car shop is a wonderful second choice. They even tolerate the clean-up, watching as the gooky cleansing material eats away the grease, and their hands emerge from the hot water spotless, except for under the nails, and wondrously worn.

It's a physical world held together by special cognitive skills and an exact, scientific language of labor, assemblage, and construction. There is music and dance and liberation in that shop, as well as an orderliness and a rather telling union of human spirit and inanimate matter. Wood is carefully touched, its straight edges lined up by eye, the timbre of metal listened for, its smoothness felt. Mouths store Phillips screws or hold the ends of string, and pockets bulge with nails, knives, tape measures, screwdrivers, and varieties of gadgets.

It's as the principal had told me: "These young men are learning a trade. It's good for them. Can't everybody go to college, you know. But this is very important for these disadvantaged youths. You'll see what I mean when you visit down there. Andy here will show you where to go. Understand you've been talking with Richmond and Fannion?"

"Yessir."

"Dangerous boys, dangerous boys. Wish we could separate them. Violent. You pick that up yet?"

"No. Not yet."

"Well, you will. Violent. Regular thing. Bad home life. No father around when the boys needed one. Always carrying knives or something. Caught Richmond last year carrying a gun. Believe that? [Absolutely not, I thought.] Fought like a bear to keep us from getting it. Had to call his mother in and everything. Trouble with these people is they don't even know what their kids are doing half the time. And if the parents can't help us out . . . I mean, they must think we're running some kind of reform school here.

"Well, Andy here will show you the way. The school's open to you, sir. I've got everything arranged. Go anywhere you like. Ask anyone anything you want to know. I won't stand in your way. I won't press you to tell me what you find out but I'd be a little curious to know. Stop in later if you have a minute."

For a long while, I had forgotten the conversation with Anthony Maggio, the principal of "Boys Tech." "Tough Tony the Gouger," Bobby had called him. "Someday, man." Phil had smiled and muttered, "motherfucker." I recall how our impressions of those boys had not been at all coincident. Just recently, however, my conversation with Anthony Maggio became vivid again, prompted by the news that five youths from "Tech" had "turned the trick" on a filling station and were now headed for a state reform school: Beatty, John R.; Walker, Lawrence J.; Cleveland, Millard L.; Richmond, Robert E.; and Fannion, Phillip R. Car shop had saved them from the rooms and teachers upstairs. Certainly it had brought us together. It had permitted them to call me "honkie" and helped me to interpret that sound, for the moment, as a label of intimacy. But not too many schools can safeguard their students, especially those schools in which constraints are vicious and omnipresent.

The police report had described Robert Richmond as "carrying a gun and violent." He was the only one of the five charged with resisting arrest and assaulting an officer. One for "Tough Tony," zero for the social scientist.

Do school personnel know their "own kind" best, or do they produce a certain kind just more "easily" knowable?

The earlier descriptions and evaluations meant more to me now, in the light of my recent experience. Each of us is an educational expert of a sort, though. We all know school or at least our own school. It is one of the few institutions that all people experience in some form. School and family. But the variations are enormous, the contrasts startling; so many teachers governed by philosophies encrusted with emotional expansiveness here, limitation there. So many people able to tolerate no more and no less than all the rest of us can tolerate.

All of us teach; all of us love telling of our work or displaying our imaginative and physical efforts. Yet, what the few schools I visited seemed to be doing was stimulating some, depressing others, rolling over indifferent others, and somehow sinking into everyone. The schools were bringing a chosen portion of a country to its pupils, which means a set of rubrics and values to preserve, and a set of ideals and consequences to arrange for at some future date. And this leaves the present which often is constituted with joy and challenge and an ethos one can only call the present for the present's sake. Often, too, the present for many students — day by day, math class by math class, or English class by English class — is nothing but a temporal vacuum, a tunnel linking a trying past to a future stale even before it is unwrapped. Still, just about every person finds the strength to crawl through, always with the hope that the end might bring pure air and a chance to stand upright, stretching for the sky.

Even more, these schools were teaching their students just how to feel about and how to comprehend the time and contents of their lives, as well as the lives shaped by their portion of the culture. Socialization, career training, and personal development are not merely heady conceptual name tags. You can see them if you care to look for them, perhaps even film them.

The key thought remains now what it has always been; the new technology and jargon of education are not fooling anyone. There is no education until people come together and experience as part of their bonding, as a clause of their charter, human care and knowledge. In the end, a sense of true welfare for everyone and a competence with a body of information, be it musical, literary, mechanical, astronomical, it makes no difference, must underlie the coincidence of lives that comprises school. At times, the needs of children and adults will demand that teachers attend to them. But apart from attending to people, education will always mean learning for personal use and growth, as well as recognizing that knowledge, information, conceptualization, indeed perceptions and taste, can be transcendent.

But if a culture, indeed if the smallest community suffers from systematic political, economic, or social oppression, a sickness is born in all institutions and in those human beings most vulnerable to illness and hurt. Let no one, however, think that children alone are the vulnerable ones. At times, their age, naiveté, and impetuosity save them, or at least provide them a resiliency no longer available to their elders.

To a great extent, the experience of school is the experiencing of culture, and although much of this experience is metaphysical or indescribable, much of it is colossally real, replicable, able to weather systematic research and personal observation. For some reason, I suspect that most of us really do understand about schools, or at least are able to conjure up images and sensations of our school days. We know that human beings are able to withstand suffering and torture. Thus, while many persons suffer from subtle and insidious injuries, barely perceptible perhaps, profound hurt is usually caused by horrendous error, trauma, insult, and dehumanization, experienced on a continual basis. What we choose to do with this knowledge and these hurts, what we elect to preserve from our schools, and what we decide to alter in them would seem to reflect, therefore, what we might wish to do with our land, with our cultural inheritance, with each other, and with the frighteningly small amount of time given each of us.

chapter nine

tomorrow
i'll
know
my
future

*suburban education
and the anxiety
of achievement*

On a trip to California I visited a handsome suburban high school where by accident — fate perhaps — I met Barbara Simpkin. Along with several friends, she shared her thoughts with me about school, what college might bring, and what her career might look like.

With all the talk about education, we often overlook suburban students and their rights, or we believe that their station in life implies that they experience no problems, no pressures, no serious concerns. Yet, what happens inside and outside their classrooms indicates that scholastic and career achievement is no simple matter. The pressures on these students are frequently as great as the opportunities society makes available to them. Implicit in the conversations in chapter nine is the fact that we are taking more seriously now the educational experiences of women, and recognizing the dangers of evaluating women's work as less important than men's work. Barbara Simpkin feels obliged to justify her talents and her belief that, despite her affluent background and prominent high school, she nevertheless deserves the rewards and career that an excellent academic record can help her to attain.

Barbara Simpkin was barefoot when we first visited together. She lay stretched out on a mat, clad in a skintight black leotard with wide straps that tucked around the bottom of her feet. Earlier I had watched as she and a class of mostly girls, but a few boys as well dressed in Levis and sweatshirts with football numbers on the back, performed routines of predance exercises. Extending and straining they blended their movement to the music, sometimes classical, like "Les Sylphides," sometimes — what would you call it? — "memorable rock," like "It's Been a Hard Day's Night" and "Norwegian Wood" played on a tinny brown upright in the corner of the gymnasium by Elsie Shapiro. Elsie was utterly marvelous, not merely because she could slip in and out of melodies, moods, and tempi according to the shifting calls and instructions of Mrs. Yarrell, not even because she could obviously compute her income tax as she played, or at least that's how I read her expressionless face, but because she could play while sipping a glass of milk with her left hand and keeping a burning cigarette between the middle and fourth fingers of her right hand.

"Yarrell and Shapiro," I was told by principal Milo Featherstone, "are permanent fixtures in this school. I wouldn't even begin to try to describe them to you. But if we ever had to let them go, this place would go up for grabs. I don't know what we're going to do when we have to retire them. The only hope for me is that I'll be long gone by then."

I took a walk past the cafeteria, the swimming pool, and the handsome boys' gym, down the concrete stairs, beyond the print shop and art studios which look out over the associated lower schools' playing fields, to the girls' gym. I entered quietly at one end. "*And* one *and* two *and* three *and* four and *breathe* and two and *three* and *four* and *stretch* and *down* and three and four and *up* and *down* and stretch Wilma Gray or your thighs will lock on you (all these words coming in just under two beats) *and* two *and* three and four and REST." And with that one word, forty-two suburban kids from fairly well-to-do California families collapsed, exhausted, on the recently shellacked gymnasium floor.

"God, she's a beautiful tyrant, isn't she?" Barbara had groaned as we left the gym some thirty minutes after that collapsing "REST." "If all of school were this way, it'd be great, wouldn't it? Maybe I should have applied to Bennington or Sarah Lawrence."

"Why didn't you?" I asked.

"I don't know." She paused to think, patting the lovely beads of sweat from her forehead with the back of her hand and then throwing back her hair with a sudden lurching but still artistic move of her head. "Well, I do know. See, the thing is, for the last three years and the first part of this year I've been wrestling with the same question. Well, it's like sociology was today. You were there. That's right. I keep forgetting you've been spying on us."

"Some spy," I defended myself.

"Well, at least you're not making movies of us like that other group that came."

"Would you like that better?" I asked.

"Hmm. Much," she responded and posed, unwittingly, for my invisible camera.

"Sociology," I prompted her.

"Oh, right. Well, we were talking about roles, women's roles, and that's really where it's at for me. I guess you could say that's my big hang-up about school. I mean, a girl has to decide, it seems to me — this is just me talking now — whether she wants to have a career. You know, use her education, or just, you know, wait around 'til she gets married."

"How do your parents feel about it?" I asked.

"Well, see, Mother doesn't really say too much, but Daddy wants me to go to college. He's told me. He's really great. He thinks women should do whatever they want to do. Go to college, be doctors and lawyers. Anything."

"Or a dancer?"

"Me? A *dancer*? You obviously weren't watching me then too closely."

"That's what *you* think. I was taking movies."

"Color or black and white?" she asked perfectly straight-faced.

Four days with Barbara Simpkin, with easily recalled dates: April 12, 13, 14, and 15. The tension around this one opulent high school was growing by the minute, at least for the seniors. April 15 would bring the notorious thick letters or thin letters; the good move-ahead-to-where-you've-been-dreaming-of news, or the depressing well-it's-too-bad-you-wasted-all-that-time-and-got-started-so-late-you-ruined-your-chances news.

I visited French III, the advanced class, with Barbara, and later sat in on an English class, "Senior Lit." In the former, a veritable taskmaster had students speaking French from start to finish. Anyone who lapsed into English was fined. *"Un nickel de plus, Michelle. C'est dommage. Mais, c'est vraiment incroyable à cette date."* They laughed at her sternness and melodramatic sense of tragedy, then went on discussing André Schwartz-Bart's gorgeous novel, *The Last of the Just.* She worked them hard, Madame Cicorel did. Her energy was staggering. Prancing about the room, shoving her face into the faces of the students who sat on the outer edges of the ring of chairs, she would glower down her twisting, bumpy nose at those whose excited stuttering and groping for a noun or idiom had turned an innocuously feminine something into an ignominiously masculine something else. She begged them to think, to create, to listen. *"Maintenant, écoutez très bien!"* Insisting on a French pronunciation of Schwartz-Bart, she watched intently the workings of the minds of those who were silent but comprehending, and then those whose faces bled puzzlement. *"Bien, Pierre. Très bien,"* she would gasp as a thought I barely could decipher finally, finally, finally made its way from the French cerebral lobes of Peter Hacklestone's overcrowded brain. *Livre de Prononciation* sat on the wide arm of his chair hiding a University of Michigan catalogue. Already accepted to Ann Arbor, he was waiting, that is to say praying, for Princeton to send him the note: *Oui, soyez le bienvenu à Princeton.*

Toward the end of the class Barbara passed me a note: "If you're bored, and I'm sure you are, leave. Madame won't mind. She probably won't even see you. Anyway, she knows you're *l'étranger.*"

"Je reste ici," I wrote back, and signed it "Thomas J. Camus." At last I was back in school. Good or bad, this was the milieu I had known. Note passing symbolized the final mark of inclusion, and strangely enough the thought of reinstatement in high school was actually rather pleasant, not at all like the anxious dreams that continue to recur now many years since my own graduation. How great school would be if they just stripped away the pressures, the untoward constraints, and retained only the joys of learning and the worth not merely of individual students, but of scholars, painters, scientists, mathematicians, novelists like Schwartz-Bart, just exactly as Madame Cicorel was doing. She was a virtuoso and her prized students, a large group of whom performed for me, were for the moment, transported. Not to France. Nothing like that; just transported into a region of their minds where wondrous capabilities lie ready for mature stimulation and actuation. They were performing; a

group of well-dressed students who looked about as French as what? the school itself, perhaps; a group of students who sounded about as French as I do when I string together my *vingt mots,* but performing nonetheless as soloists who loved their music and, most amazing, saw no reason to be competitive.

That was it! They were piecing together this difficult score and for once, perhaps, not begrudging anyone else's "native talents" or hard-earned accomplishments, and not disparaging anyone else's seemingly pathetic lack of feel for a subject. What this dynamo bolting back and forth in front of us had done over the last three years was now visible, for irrespective of the performance quality of it all, the experience in fact *was* admirable. That is, Horowitz may be performing, but the sound, the result is still out of this world. And these young people were sensational. A great teacher had raised their sense of esteem and assessment of their own propensities to an extraordinary height, a height maybe possibly only because of the underlying foreignness of the topic. And yet, as "high" as they were, she had nonetheless rendered French literature so noble, so royal, that it actually shone above these glorious people, ascendant and supreme.

Knowledge and a simple human being's capacity for it were the products of these four times a week meetings now coming to their conclusion. But even as the star, Madame Cicorel, who every day commuted eighteen miles to this school because on her simple wage there was no place for her to live in the community or immediately surrounding communities, was also subjugated by the language and literature of the French. She, too, was subjugated by the "irregularities" of social and linguistic form and the fact that no one had the chance to practice anything with real Frenchmen as there were none around, except for an occasional domestic or shopkeeper, or until one traveled to Montreal. Despite the fact, too, that France and everything called French just do not inspire a lot of American teenagers, unless of course one speaks of some painters, Killy, the Follies, Montand maybe, Aznavour maybe, Sartre and Camus, and of course that string of movie people. But even here the name of Jeanne Moreau was not recognized by many students, and Resnais by even fewer.

In English class, the opposite reigned, and the movie cameras everywhere, particularly those in the students' minds, clicked off. Nothing at all seemed worth preserving. The only notes taken by anyone dealt with homework assignments for the following Monday. They were "bulling their way" through poetry of E. E. Cummings in anticipation of reading Alan Ginsberg the following week. But nothing was coming together. You could see minds turning off. Postures oozed tedium and anxiety. It was low-key, routine, emotionless, lifeless, a lull before another lull, and all so different from Yarrell, Shapiro, and Cicorel, the "beauteous tyrants" or "beatitudes" or whatever Barbara had called them. Mr. McArthur was turning these young people aside even as he strip mined the capital-less first lines of Cummings. The questions he asked, though reasonable, were stifling the students in their predictability and perfunctoriness. He was behaving in a standard academic way, and the transparency of his didactic motives and purposes was, I suppose, driving them crazy — not that their own responses were so tantalizing.

The scene was becoming too difficult to judge, as the interactions between adult, young people, and E. E. Cummings were grinding to a nowhere. When would the class bell ring? Had it broken or something? Had the mystical timekeeper who sits in a mountain in Colorado or Vermont or Peru and punches the school bells in every corridor in America at 11:50 and 1:24 and 9:36 finally fallen asleep? Ring already, I've had enough here.

"What did I tell you?" came Barbara's note. "Is this the worst, ever? Tomorrow at this time I'll know my future."

"Help," I wrote back. Then, "You will be successful, Lady Fair. Have no doubts." She smiled when she read my words. Oh, for one look inside her head. Just to know the tensions and excitement of high school, of being seventeen years old; of the billion hours of studying, the notes in class, about class, for after class; of the trillion Sunday nights and last days of vacations when work isn't done and those pangs of pain that signal a recognition that the work will not get done. And of all the ideas about career, and steady and unsteady academic, social, and psychic progress, and steady and unsteady dating.

To listen to Barbara and her friends in Stillman cafeteria was to realize that the line dividing present preoccupations and future adventure, chance, even fame, is very thin indeed. It was not the case that these young people calculated each moment only in terms of unseen future payments. They were playing games of school, indeed games of fortune, but a sizable investment was being made in day-by-day efforts and enterprises. The senior play, *Ring Around the Moon*, for example, had brought forth envies, sorrow, and personal beauty from a small group of dedicated actors who only occasionally spoke the language of extracurricular activities and college preparation.

A certain segment of life was about to end for these seniors. College boards and other preparative necessities were behind them, "Thank God!" But so, too, were splendid hours not only with the dynamos, but on the athletic fields, in classes and study halls, in student government meeting chambers, and in hushed dark rooms with a date. No one recounts earliest intimacies on college applications. No one yet lists first cigarettes, first trials with pot, a go with speed maybe, or missed menstrual periods which for an instant mean horror, despite all the modern slogans and calls for personal liberation. No one lists private victories and defeats on college applications where it says: "State what you believe to be your outstanding assets and liabilities."

"Well, what *did* I write?" Harvey Swoboda munched on a sandwich, his arm around the girl who owned the silver basketball he had earned. "My greatest asset is my beautiful bod, and my greatest liability is that Laurie Mannis won't let me use it with other girls."

"Harvey, you obscene pig. Take your stinking arm off of me." The students were roaring, choking, coughing, and "Harves" was dramatically perched on stage. A dusty shaft of light spun through a crack between the edge of the window shade and the frame, and had he hunched forward a foot or so he would have received his spotlight.

"Oh, it's true. How many girls have come to you asking for my hot bod? Tell 'em."

"Jesus. You're a despicable slime."

"A despicable slime she calls me. I'm only listing my assets and liabilities for the man. I don't even care if he goes back to Harvard and tells them what I said because the letter's in the mail, man. It's all over now." They became quiet suddenly, very quiet indeed for a group of people interested in the media; two fellows from the school ham radio club, three from the newspaper, and one each from the literary magazine, underground press, and yearbook. Some of the best students in this school had taken time to visit with me on the eve of their own national elections, their own heavyweight bout with "the establishment." American society, which had taken quite a rap in the mouth yesterday during what in this school is called American Studies, was coming out all right today at lunch. In my mind I filmed them as athletes, the boys as well as the girls, sitting on the bench waiting for the coach to call upon them. Or maybe they were young teenagers in the early forties, hushed in a circle around a cheap, crackling radio, a distant newsman giving them the latest information on the war and, more importantly, on what the outcome of today's battles would mean for their own private destinies. So where was all the infamous social change? Nothing was different on my own special April 14, ten thousand years before.

I slept extremely well on the fourteenth. Barbara dreamed that all six schools to which she applied had said "No." Their letters had been cordial, she reported, but unequivocal. I regret to inform you . . . there were so many outstanding candidates this year. . . . We wish you luck elsewhere. . . . Then, on the afternoon of the fifteenth, we got a ride to her house from a quiet junior boy on the track team. The letters were there waiting. Her mother had phoned the school. A million parents had phoned a million schools.

"I know now exactly what my conflict has been," Barbara was saying. "College or marriage isn't it at all. I've never been able to say how much I wanted to go to college, to one of these six best of all. I've tried to hide it from the boys I date, and most of the girls, and I suppose, in a way, from my parents." At the door of her house she paused and looked at me. "No matter what happens I want to go to college, and I worked for it as hard as I could. No scholarships, no honors, but I do want them to accept me now more than anything else."

"Good luck," I mumbled.

"Oh, God, I'm so nervous I think I'm going to die." Inside the handsome vestibule of the large suburban house, on top of a sleek, rosewood cabinet the morning's mail lay in two piles; one group for the family — I remember a copy of *Life* there — and a second group of envelopes marked "Miss Barbara Andrea Simpkin."

"Listen," I said, "I'm getting so nervous myself I wish you'd just open them already."

"Would you mind if I took them upstairs to my bedroom? Just in case."

"Of course. Of course."

"MOTHER," she screamed.

"I'm upstairs, dear. I know. What's the verdict?" came from above. Barbara grabbed the letters, felt them, and pretended to weigh them for me. Then she held them up to the light. "Are they too thin?" Then she darted upstairs, for an instant a seven-year-old girl hunting frantically for a lost toy. A door slammed and her mother called her name. At last the house was silent. Behind a louvered door, in the kitchen presumably, the motor of the refrigerator turned over. Still no sound from above. The motor stopped. A plane flew overhead, its engines dull and gravelly.

At last an upstairs door opened and I peered upward as though one might actually be able to see through eight inches of ceiling beams and plaster. Barbara was speaking softly to her mother. I thought I heard Mrs. Simpkin say something like, "Bless you, dear, I'm so proud." Then sound on the stairs and there she was. Her appearance seemed as before, after-school-slightly-disheveled, but tears gushed from her eyes, her mascara running rivulets of fluid and soot, blue and black, down her cheeks. Her face was reddened and moist. She was smiling, then laughing and crying both as only girls, I think, can do. She looked at me as though I had been the author of the news and these newest feelings as well.

"I've been accepted all over. Everywhere except Reed and I didn't want to go there anyway. I don't know why I'm crying." And as she started down the stairs muttering something about all the people she had to telephone, "Daddy, Uncle Jack, Sally Alexander, oh, and Madame," she reached her arms out to me. From my angle beneath her I saw her legs and the lower part of her body filter in and out of the spindles holding the balustrade. I moved to the bottom of the stairs to welcome her, my four-day-old friend. Our fingers were almost touching now. "You won't be mad at me if I choose Yale?"

chapter ten

we're born dumb hillbillies

*educational testing
and the power
of intelligence*

Sitting in my office one day, I heard the voices of several people outside in the corridor. At once I recognized those special sounds that characterize people from Appalachia. Among the group was Hindi Buchanan with whom, all told, I have spoken for less than five hours.

The major issue in chapter ten is educational testing, and more precisely, intelligence testing. Although none of us would draw identical pictures of school nor recount identical educational experiences, most of us would place testing and intelligence in our pictures and accounts. Even if we fight against our temptation to differentiate people by test scores or by their I.Q.'s, these distinctions continue to emerge in our visions and assessments of schools and students. The conversations in chapter ten consider the use and validity of intelligence tests and of educational testing generally. They show, moreover, how the values, status, and findings of educational experts affect young people's self-conceptions and ways of understanding the world. Presently, intelligence tests seem to have assumed such importance that few teachers can convince their students that the test could be culturally biased or employed for political as well as educational purposes.

A long-distance phone call alerted me to the publication of Harvard Professor Richard Herrnstein's article "I.Q." in the September 1971 issue of *The Atlantic*. "You see it yet?" my friend inquired. "Here we go again." The article, a long and cogently written one at that, turned out to be a more eloquent restatement of a position Professor Arthur Jensen had published many months before in the *Harvard Educational Review*. Both men had drawn together an impressive collection of studies in which intelligence tests were administered to black and white schoolchildren and had come to the conclusion that a certain significant degree of intelligence, as measured by existing tests, could indeed be attributed to an inheritability factor. More precisely, the distribution of intelligence scores which showed black children with lower I.Q.'s than white children seemed to indicate for Professors Jensen and Herrnstein that a certain portion of human variation is due to native ability and not environment, native ability that contributes to a stratification of human groups predicated on intelligence.

To some people, the Herrnstein article, now legitimated in a new way by its publication in a popular rather than an academic journal, meant that blacks were born dumber than whites and would therefore have to acknowledge this newly discovered genetic basis for their inferior social standing. To others, Herrnstein was a despicable racist. Others objected to the criticism of the article, claiming that Herrnstein's data and reasoning were sound, thoughtful, scholarly, and open to mature debate. Others who had brought forth data and had written arguments against the genetic and statistical inadequacies in Jensen's notion of inheritability began to crank up for still another attack on an issue they hoped might have been settled. Once again, the old warhorse of nature versus nurture, biological or sociological determinism, had come back to tantalize psychologists, and as always, the political implications of the debate seemed unavoidable.

Cambridge dinner party discussions inevitably turned to the Herrnstein article, its politics, its courage, its dangers, its psychology. Some of the students in Professor Herrnstein's course, claiming that he was teaching openly racist materials, protested to such an extent that a university-wide petition was passed around deploring the lack of academic freedom shown him. Professors insisted that the students cease harassing their colleague. Signing the petition were many professors who, though they opposed the Herrnstein article and were in the process of writing rejoinders, felt nonetheless that academic freedom had to be preserved. Not signing the petition was a man who argued, interestingly, that controversial presentations in the popular press do not give a professor the right to claim academic freedom in his classroom. And finally, there were the letters, the inevitable confetti that swirls about the parade of debate. One black person approved of the Herrnstein article and some whites were horrified. Another black person made mention of Hitler and the gas chambers and other whites were horrified. Some people offered qualifications, some people offered substantiating evidence, pro or con, some offered their congratulations, some lacked sufficient credentials even to have their letters published.

Around Boston anyway, people were debating. The academic community which had for so long devised and sanctioned intelligence testing was now debating intelligence quotients and their implications. In the poor areas around Boston, however, where I do my own research, listening to people describing poverty and the strains of day-by-day survival and seeking to bring these descriptions, these lives, to the very people who might have been convinced by the Herrnstein article, I heard no debates. I continued to hear from black mothers and fathers requests to prepare their children for taking intelligence tests. For I.Q. scores are no longer data or even currency in these areas, they are an element in the blood, peculiarly shaped cells that a child better have a lot of if he or she is going to survive beyond grade school and high school. It was the existence of these cells that I found missing in the debates in which I myself participated. People, not just their ideas or their political positions, were being attacked and hurt. People who have never been able to afford debate were feeling something in their bodies, still another force of opposition, still another reminder of their status and with it their destiny. All people feel these periodic waves that emanate from the scientific community. People in the urban ghettos feel these waves that threaten their sense of self, identity, and possibility. People from the hollows of West Virginia do too, even though it may seem to some of us that a particular wave is directed toward a very different group of people. But a young woman whom I met quite accidentally, someone whose world and sense of history are different from my own, reminded me of the power of science and of universities, and of how quickly the ideas of one person can touch the soul of another person, although the two will never meet.

A small group of students from a college in eastern Kentucky was traveling in New England at the time that the leaves began to change. I never learned, exactly, the details of their mission, but in the Boston area they were visiting several universities and, I must say, looking rather wide-eyed at the proportions of our city and educational plants. Hindi Buchanan, who spoke with a gentle accent — she claimed my own Chicago-bred tones were rather fierce — seemed surprised that I would know some of the small towns around Morgantown and Wheeling, West Virginia, where she and the clusters of her family were born and still live.

"Know the Washton family in Wheeling?" I smiled at her. She grinned back.

"Name-dropper. Do you know the Hackneys, or the Twylers, or the Perwaggys, or the Borowys, or the Buchanans, for that matter?"

I looked at her seriously. She is tall with smooth blue-black hair that falls freely about her face. Her skin is impure, and she uses her hair to hide her cheeks and forehead. Her eyes are a deep brown, her nose straight, her lips thin and dry. She is embarrassed, it would seem, by her height, and so she slumps in a way that lifts her abdomen and brings her shoulders down and closer together.

"No. Those names don't ring a bell, but I hear tell that the Twylers and the Perwaggys have been feuding for years."

"Don't laugh. The Perwaggys have a son who tried to kill some boy once just for going out with his sister."

"My God. Is that true?"

"Sure. All that stuff people up here make believe about us hillbillies," she said the word with derision, "has some truth to it, you know. We got all sorts of family feuds going on. Guys with beards up in the hills . . ."

"In the hollows," I interrupted her, if only to inform her of my own travels.

"Oh, now that's good. That's the right word. You've visited in Virginia and Kentucky, then, if you know about the hollows. Well, anyway, we got these men with beards and rifles picking each other off so that they can square all their bets and feuds. Take their revenge, and all of that."

"Yeah, I'll bet you have. We have them too."

"Don't I know. Hey, can I sit down?" Hindi looked about at the furniture and walls of my small office. The pictures of children, especially, pleased her. Turning on the secretarial stool, she examined a photograph of a young boy, a trouble-shooting eleven-year-old from East Cambridge. She smiled. "I like him. What's his name? You know?"

"Philly. Phillip William Barnstable. The kids call him 'Stable Boy.'"

"I like it that his shirt is torn. That makes it believable to me, somehow. You see there the way he's unaware of his sleeve?" The photograph shows Stable Boy standing, resting his chin on his left hand. The cuff of his long-sleeved polo shirt is shredded. "That's what makes it real for me. Stable Boy. He could be from Morgantown. There are a lot of boys there who look just like him, with torn shirts, and torn hearts, too, I suppose." Hindi turned back to look at me. I said nothing. "What's the matter?" she asked.

"Oh, I guess I was admiring your poetic way."

"You take the photograph?" Hindi asked.

"I did, yes. I'm not good, but I once thought I'd . . ."

"You're good. *You're* poetic too."

"Thank you, ma'am."

"Hindi."

"Thank you, Hindi." I nodded acceptance of her correction. She was again looking hard at me in a way that made it impossible for me to turn away.

"You think a lot, don't you?" she observed.

"Yes. So do you, I imagine."

"Not that much really. Visiting up here I seem to do a lot more. I think that thinking is a protection for me. It's like I'm standing guard when I'm thinking. No, maybe it's that when I'm aware that I'm thinking I know that everything around me isn't totally friendly."

"Where did you go to school, Hindi?"

"Oh, a typical place in Morgantown. You never heard of it."

"D'you like it?"

"No. Not really. I liked some of the students. Oh," she shook her head, "I don't want to talk about things like that. Where did *you* go to school?"

"A small school in Chicago."

"*You* like it?"

"Yes."

"Why?" She was grinning.

"Well, that's a good question. I guess because, oh brother, you've got me trying so hard now to give you a poetic answer."

"Go on. Because . . ."

"Because, I suppose, I felt they cared for me and made me feel worthy or worth, or whatever the word is."

"They didn't at my school. I never felt that anyone cared about me. 'Cause I'm not pretty I didn't even get *that* kind of attention. I never felt worthy or worth. What is the word? Worthy?"

"Right. I think. Did some of the kids there make a distinction between, you know, city kids and rural kids?"

"You don't have to be so careful, Dr. Cottle."

"Tom."

"Tom. Of course they did. They still do distinguish between city people and the families from the creeks and the mountains and mining regions. You better believe they distinguish plenty." All this time she continued to stare at me. Never did she look away or read the lines of emptiness with her eyes as one does in searching for next thoughts or recollections. "They had all kinds of distinctions when I lived there. I learned them when I was a girl. My Pa told me never to mind them, just to live with dignity and believe in the Lord and all that stuff, but you don't forget what you learn from your peers."

"Like what?"

"Like the fact that eastern people or northern or city people are smart, and that folks like us are, well, sort of dumb. From the Stone Age, museum examples, like. You know what I mean."

"Hmm."

"Don't look so sad about it. We're making it. Some of us, anyway. I'm in college along with a slew of other young people. It's not M.I.T., of course, but we're making it. People can think what they like. Strange, though, that I say that."

"What's that?" I asked.

"Oh, I guess I'm sounding a lot like my mother. I always remember her saying things to me and my brothers like, 'Let people think what they like. You can't ever change people's minds. You can only improve yourself. That's the only thing that matters.' Stuff like that. I never thought I'd be quoting her."

"Is your mother alive?" I believed, somehow, from the reverence in Hindi's words that she was not.

"No. My mother died when I was ten. She'd had tuberculosis for a long time. She was always sick. As long as I can remember. Her mother had it too. Neither of them lived beyond thirty-five. My mother was thirty-three, almost thirty-four. I guess that's maybe another one of those distinctions, you know. We die sooner in the mountains than the people in the city. Did you ever hear of black lung disease?"

"Yes, I have."

"Well, that's part of the same thing. The differences, I mean. There are lots of illnesses that are never treated. I think that mountain people, even the people in my family, always want to deny that something is wrong with them when they get sick or something horrible happens. I think they do."

"But many people do that."

"Well, maybe they do. I guess so. But what I've seen growing up, seems like these people constantly pretend things are better than they are. My Pa always said that things have to get better. 'If a person works hard, they get better; God listens to you only when you're working,' he always says. Or loving, too, I suppose."

"He's not dead, though?"

"No. He's alive." Hindi relaxed in her chair. "I think I'm giving you the impression that my life has been one tragedy after another. It really hasn't. Actually, it's been like everyone else's life. I'm not that special," she smiled at me. "I'm really not. You can see that by looking at me. I'm not that special."

"God, I feel like *you're* comforting *me*," I replied, "and I'm supposed to be your host here."

"You're not my host. You're just somebody new." She looked at her watch.

"Do you have to go?" I asked.

"You busy?"

"Nope."

"You're lying."

"No. I'm not. You late for the next thing in your visit?"

"No. I was just thinking that I've known you less than ten minutes and I've already told you that my mother died. That's some kind of a record for me, I think."

"Good. Or, well, I'm honored."

"All right," she said after moments of silence, "feel honored."

"I have a bit of a nagging feeling," I started, "that I came on a little strong about wanting to show you I know a little bit about your home area. You know?"

"Oh, I'm used to that. Lots of people up here do that same thing with us. That doesn't make you special or anything. I'm not bothered by that."

"Well, O.K. I just wanted to let you know I've been in West Virginia."

"Me too," she grinned, "I've been there too. Now I'm here. So what? People are still people. We're all about the same, I suppose." For the first time since examining the photographs Hindi turned away from me, swiveling on the secretarial stool to investigate my bookshelf and the small collection of magazines and journals. "What have you got that I should read?"

"Anything there you'd like. Take your pick."

"What's this like?" The word *Politics*, printed vertically in blue letters, showed on a paperback. "Oh, Israel," she exclaimed, yanking the rest of the book from under a pile of papers and discovering author Leonard Fein's name as well. "I'm not ready for Israel yet. What's this? *Psychology Today*. Is this any good?"

"Not bad. There's always an interesting article . . ." She had already put the magazine down and was fingering something else.

"*Journal of Experimental Social Psychology.*" She said the words slowly, as if in disbelief that the English language could yield such sounds. "You actually read this?" she asked incredulously, scanning some of the pages.

"Once upon a time," I responded sheepishly.

"But no more."

"Not too much."

"Good. That settles that. You don't mind me checking you out through your books, do you?" She never bothered to look back at me.

"Nope. Check away."

"Now then, *The Foundation Directory*. Edition Three. Marianna O. Lewis, Editor. Analytical Introduction by F. Emerson Andrews. That must be exciting."

"Don't laugh. That may be my most valuable book. In fact, now that you remind me, I'm going to take that home with me tonight."

"Someone might steal it, eh?" Hindi ran her fingers across other books and pamphlets, supporting fallen books with piles of articles. "What you need is someone to come in and clean up once in a while for you. Look how these are." She inspected her hands.

"Hmmm. A maid. That's all I need."

"A maid," she repeated. "Hey, look at this. I've heard about this." She turned to face me. "Let me . . . can I borrow this? I'll bring it back."

"What have you got?"

"This, here. *The Atlantic* with that I.Q. business article. Is it yours? Can I take it? I'll bring it back. Today, ah, day after tomorrow? O.K.? We'll be here for a week more."

"Of course. Take it. Keep it."

"No, I don't want to keep it. I just want to borrow it. Is it long?" She fingered through the pages of the issue until she reached the table of contents. Then she scanned page after page of the lengthy article by Professor Richard Herrnstein.

"Take it, Hindi. Please."

"No." She was earnest about not owning the copy of the magazine. Disgust and pain shown on her face when she realized the article's length. "Ugh. Such small print, too." She shook her head from side to side. "I'm going to do it. Everybody here's been talking about this; I guess I have to read it. Day after tomorrow, right?"

"Day after tomorrow. Hey Hindi, let's make a date when you bring it back. Maybe we could talk about it then."

"Oh, that's cool. You read it?"

"Parts of it. But I'll prepare for you."

"But you won't have a copy if I take yours. Here, you keep this one, I'll get another."

I threw her a don't-be-silly look. "I've got another copy at home."

"You sure? Really?"

"Don't you trust me, West Virginia?" I grinned at her.

"You born in a city of over five hundred people?"

"Yeah. Chicago."

"Then I don't trust you, but I'll keep your crumby magazine." Like a schoolgirl, she held the copy of *The Atlantic* with both hands against her breasts. She saw me looking at the magazine which now seemed so protected. Herrnstein and all the fortunate writers of this one issue were now being well kept. She looked down at the magazine. "I'll take good care of it," she promised. Turning the magazine over and rotating it right side up, she cradled it to her body again. The word *Atlantic* peeped over her arms.

"Wednesday," she said as she turned to leave. "Find me some other books too. O.K.? Or magazines. But not the . . . *The Foundation*—" We said "*Directory*" in unison. Upon reaching the outer office she stopped, and now, out of the line of my vision, called back to me:

"What time on Wednesday?"

"Afternoon? Threeish?"

"Threeish? Boy, you *are* big city."

"Three o'clock sharp, Miss Buchanan," I corrected myself. I heard her laugh and I smiled. As she left the outer door to enter the main corridor I heard her counting: "Threeish, fourish, fivish . . ."

Hindi returned two days later, wearing the same clothes and looking a bit more tired. She walked directly to the stool on which she had sat before and rolled it closer to the desk. The copy of *The Atlantic* lay in her lap, her hands, palms down, on top of it. "Well, what do you want to talk about?" she asked.

"What do *I* . . . ? Well, I thought we'd talk about the article, but we don't have to. I'd just as soon talk about you."

"Or *you*."

"Or me, though I think you're more . . ."

"Oh, God," she blurted out. In an instant, looking directly at me, she had suddenly begun to cry, her hands rising reflexively to cup her eyes over her glasses. "I didn't want to cry." Tears fell behind the lenses into the heels of her hands. "Damn. Damn me. I'm a child."

"What's wrong, Hindi? Hey, you can cry in here." I rose to shut the door and cursed the thin walls that would not protect our voices. "Want to tell me?"

"It's this. Moving her body forward, she bumped the magazine in her lap with her elbows. "This. Mr., Professor Herrnstein."

"What did he say?"

"Didn't you read it?" She was sniffling. "You said you'd read it, too."

"I did. I did. What is it?" My inquiry only made her weep more. I waited for her. When she spoke, her words were interrupted by her crying:

"He says so much. I know. I mean, he knows about black people and their intelligence, and it's horrible that they, that they are so, so, oh help me."

"That blacks are supposedly born different?"

"Different? He says they're not intelligent or that they are inheriting, you know, different from the whites."

"I don't believe it for a minute," I replied.

"But it's true. He wouldn't lie. He's a Harvard professor. He wouldn't lie. He can't lie. He's studied this and he knows. You must know that. He's at Harvard. That means everything, and he knows."

"But the data can be argued, and the notion of inheritability is misinterpreted all over the place. It's not scientific!"

"No! I don't believe it," she insisted, still sobbing.

"Hindi. You cannot read that article as being absolute truth. We went all through this with another guy once, and hundreds of people wrote papers opposing his position. Good people. Just as good and informed. They fought it."

"No!" She screamed the word at me. "It's true. It's all true. I know it. I know it just from talking with you. You're smarter. You all are smarter. I hear you. I see you. I've heard all these people since we've been here, and they're smarter. You know that! Professor Herrnstein is just one of the only people who's not afraid to say it right out so that people know it. Like, so that they'll have to face it. Once and for all."

"That's a lot of crap!"

"It's not!" She yelled back at me, at last looking up. "It's not crap.

You don't have anything to face like this. You couldn't possibly know. He's a Harvard professor and an expert, so it's the truth. It's all the truth. You're denying it to make me feel good."

"Hindi. That's absurd. What do you want from me? I oppose that article with all my strength."

"I don't want anything from you but to admit that it's true. Pretty soon when everyone in this country can begin to admit just who's intelligent and just who isn't, some other Harvard professor, or M.I.T. professor, like you, will come to West Virginia or Kentucky and Virginia and Pennsylvania and all over, and start to give those tests to all the schoolchildren back there, and then you'll see. You'll see what they'll find."

"What? What will I see? What are they going to find that you're so sure about with tests that rich whites design and still don't understand." I tried to control my anger. "Really. I'm serious." She barely heard me. Momentarily her voice had quieted.

"They'll find that we're dumb too. Dumber even than the black children in the schools."

"Hindi, c'mon." I reached for her hand, but she pulled away. The stool squeaked. Again her voice was loud and authoritative.

"No. They will! I went to school with black children, and we're dumber than they are. Much dumber. You don't know the children I do from the hills." The tears poured down her face. "I know them. They're part of my family. I grew up there with them. Not Chicago. They're my children. My children. I was once a child there. Don't you see that? Why do you keep forgetting that? I know exactly how smart they are. And when they have to take those tests they'll find they can't even read the instructions. They can't read. They can't read. They're born dumb. They're born stupid and ugly and dumb, and they'll test them and everyone will know it. Don't you see that?"

"No, I don't. That's preposterous. Literacy has nothing to do . . ."

"Yes. Yes. Yes. Yes. It does. It does."

"Hindi, please don't cry." My words sounded so pathetic. I looked at the walls wondering whether anyone was listening to us.

"I can't help it. It's just that it's all so painful. They'll test us next. You read all that stuff." She motioned backward with her shoulder in the direction of the bookcase. "The Journal of . . . whatever that was,

Psychology. Social Psychology. You read that stuff. Maybe it will be *you* they pick to come to Morgantown to go to the public schools and test the children. Us. Test us, I mean."

"Never! You're wrong."

"Maybe though. Maybe. Maybe you will write in this magazine someday and tell everyone. Somebody has to. You can't keep hiding everything forever, you know. Somebody has to tell."

"They don't. Hindi, c'mon. Please."

"No. They do. Somebody has to tell. They'll test those dumb dirty children from the hills, all the hillbillies, and they'll all score two and four and ten and they'll never let us come out. They'll lock us in the hills, or in those rotten neighborhoods, just like they lock the blacks in the ghettos of every city. And they'll tell us we can't come out until we can read and do arithmetic and be intelligent like you. Just like you!" She nodded her face at me.

"That's a ghastly thought."

"It's a ghastly truth. It's a ghastly truth, you mean. That's what you really mean. We're dumb. We're all dumb. I hear, I see, I talk with them. My father is so dumb you wouldn't believe it. He couldn't get past the first page of that intelligence test. My mother either. We're hillbillies! Born dumb hillbillies, and we're the next to be tested." She slammed her hands down on the magazine. "We're next! We're next. Maybe they'll get the Indians first, but you can be plain sure that we'll be next. He wouldn't lie. So don't you lie, either."

"Hindi, please, we've got so much to talk about." I held my hands out to her. She looked at me though not in the direct way she had two days before.

"I'll talk," she began softly, "but you have to promise me you won't lie."

"I promise," I said as quickly as I could.

"And you must admit it's true."

"Never. Never, ever," I responded quietly.

"Then I can never trust you. You patronize me. You do. I should kill myself for telling you about my mother. You didn't deserve it. You tricked me. Here. Take your damn magazine back. Maybe you better read it again, and maybe you better come to Appalachia and meet my folks and talk to those children, too. It might open your eyes, and put

We're Born Dumb Hillbillies   185

an end to all your dreams and all your fuzzy wishing ways of thinking about us. You may be a social scientist and all that, but you'll see that in the end I'm right. Like Professor Herrnstein is right, too. When they finish with all their testing you will see how I was right, and how we'll have to stay where we are, up in the hills and all, as bad as it is or as good as it is. It doesn't even matter at all anymore. Then you will feel shame. You'll see. Then you'll feel shame too."

Suddenly, she sat up tall in the awkward chair, her posture showing pride and assuredness: "You may even cry, then, doctor."

chapter eleven

city
teacher

*classroom authority
and the rights
of teachers*

My introduction to Elaine Bottomly, Miss Bottomly to her sixth-grade pupils, came about as a result of a small study that I undertook. Upon gaining entrance to a Boston grammar school, I asked several administrators and teachers, Who are the best teachers in the school? Elaine Bottomly's name came up again and again, and so I sought her out.

The conversation in chapter eleven offers an invaluable perspective on education. Paradoxically, teachers seem to be simultaneously overlooked and overstudied. Either way, their rights and privileges are often disparaged, and their status maligned. Some of us are critical of America's teachers; others of us tend to overromanticize their work and social position. Inevitably, though, we look more kindly on the young than on their teachers, arguing that children are innocent and naive, whereas adults are well-formed, purposeful, and resigned. The constraints, however, on teachers' behavior both inside and outside their classrooms can be ferocious, and their interactions, consequently, with students and colleagues strained and unproductive. Students often forget about these constraints and the fact that the private and public worlds of their teachers are continually being scrutinized.

The country's politics and social values as well as its

economic system and labor regulations converge to form the background for a conversation with a teacher. They affect, moreover, the dynamics in any classroom, as well as the theories and philosophies that govern teacher-training programs and the granting of educational degrees and credentials.

I first met Elaine Bottomly four years ago. After going through several weeks of meetings and interviews with school board members, district superintendents, and then the school's principal and two assistant principals, I was finally permitted to observe some of her classes in session. Elaine Bottomly, the head sixth-grade teacher of the Danvers School in the middle of Boston, waited for me at the door to her homeroom. I could tell by her tone as we exchanged greetings that I was not the first visitor to her class. She blew out a long breath before going through a checklist of items that clearly she had enumerated for everyone else who had requested permission to observe her teaching.

"Don't smoke, and if you have to take notes do it inconspicuously. I may call upon you, introduce you, you know, so be prepared for that too. What do I call you? Doctor? Professor?"

"Tom will do."

"Okay. Tom. What else? Save your questions for later and I'll do the best I can to answer them." I tried to make her see that I was sympathetic with the burdens of teachers and knew that visitors only added to their daily grief, and she noticed. I even offered to speak with her after class and forego the observations. "No, you're here. May as well see the children. Let them see you." Then she shook her head as if to say, sometimes life's just too much for any one person. At the same time she said, and with pride, "I'll tell you something. This business of having a reputation as a good teacher is beginning to bug me. It was better in the old days when nobody even noticed you." Then she laughed out loud. Walking into the main corridor, I saw her scratch the side of her head and heard her mutter: "What the hell you talking about, Elaine? When, pray tell, have you ever *not* been noticed?"

At twenty-eight, Elaine Bottomly was in her sixth year of teaching. A graduate of a teachers college in Pennsylvania, her first job had been in an inner-city grammar school in Philadelphia. There she taught black and white as well as some Spanish-speaking students. After two years she moved to Boston where she taught in a suburban grammar school fifteen miles from where she lived in the city. For three years she taught primarily white students, although the Boston busing program managed to transport several black and Oriental children into her fifth- and sixth-grade classes. As one of seven black teachers in the grammar school system, she was noticed plenty during those years.

"I'll tell you what saved me," she told me when our friendship was three years old. "I was a dish. I was more than a black. I was a piece for the bosses and the fathers. Credentials had nothing to do with it. They could have hired a million people like me. They knew it. I knew it. I remember when they brought me in for interviews. I could see it in their faces. I almost reminded them at one point, I think with an assistant principal, that it was my intention to be a teacher, and a good one, not a hat-check girl somewhere."

"You say something?" I asked.

"Yeah, sure," she answered sarcastically. "I gave a speech on women's rights. Of *course* I didn't say anything. I wanted the job. You want a job, you keep your mouth shut and your hemlines properly high." She caught me smiling. "You're one of 'em. You're just like all the rest of 'em. I'll bet you've been thinking what they're thinking all the time."

"Which is?"

"Don't you play coy. Which is, how come I didn't have a sixth-grade teacher like you."

"I've never thought that once."

"You're a liar," she responded.

"I am."

She laughed. "See. I told you. There you are, another one."

In recent years, my conversations with Elaine Bottomly have gone more easily than they did in the beginning. On my first visit, when I felt her bitterness and pride, as well as her sense of humor and always that burden she carried, I took her manner to be a challenge. "The main thing you do with me," she had said, "is take notes. I don't want you to rely on memory when it comes to the things I have to say. I don't believe in memory. Anyway, what I have to tell you is too important to allow you to make interpretations. So you get your notebook there out, and when I tell you something, you take it down verbatim. I don't care whether you publish it or not, but if you do, it had better be accurate. I mean it. This business with interviewing teachers in ghetto schools has become a racket and I'm not about to be a part of it."

"What do you mean racket?" We were headed toward the school's cafeteria. On the way she said hello by name to almost everyone we passed.

"You all come into the schools," she began, "because the media and politicians and especially you social scientists have found some new sorts of victims or heroes in the urban schools. At least this year we make interesting source material. I read what you guys write. I read it."

"And?" As if her way of speaking didn't tell me what was coming.

"Most of it makes me sick."

"Isn't it true?"

"Some is, most isn't. They either don't stay in schools long enough to know people, or they paint the pictures of high school teachers so outrageously wrong. I know teachers who can't even recognize themselves after you people get through with them. They're so much bigger than life. They're supposed to be suffering all the time, bleeding hearts, you know, getting themselves all involved with race and drugs and revolution. You people have fantasy dictating your vision. That's one of your problems. If you could remove the fantasies you might be able to see what's going on in places like this."

I was, of course, put on the defensive. But I had also been a victim of my own prejudgments. As a common practice in visiting schools, I will ask teachers, administrators, and students to list the best teachers. Despite what many people now think, there are thousands of extraordinary teachers in thousands of American schools, and if in saying this I sound like an apologist for an educational system that I cannot always support, then so be it. Every school has its great ones; they are known, even after being in the school for less than a year. They possess tangible reputations and histories, and everyone has a story about them. In this one Boston school, the name of Miss Elaine Bottomly came at me every-where I turned. My mistake was believing that the administration, in particular, had given me the name of someone who would put me at ease and make the task of interviewing easy. They had not. They had merely responded literally to my question: "Think you can say who the best teacher around here is?"

"Elaine Bottomly. She's the best we have," came their replies. "You can go a long way before you find one any better."

Elaine herself would remind me on several occasions that she was not an "open" person. "I'm not about to lay my life open for anyone from the press. Once I kind of thought I would like being interviewed, but now there's just too much of that going on. Everyone has to make public declarations about everything he does. You try something neat in class and you're lucky not to have some education school breathing down your neck the next morning. Which reminds me, why *are* you here?" I explained to her my research in the poor areas of Boston and my interest in learning about the lives of people who live and work in these areas. My explanations are always dreadfully inadequate and plain-sounding. While making observations and taking notes I feel sufficiently comfortable with the task, but when I am asked what I really am doing I normally feel incompetent and lost. Probably I communicate this to those I speak with in the form of an appeal for help.

Miss Bottomly did not respond to this appeal. In the first few months she would stare at me across the cafeteria table or in the teachers' lounge as if to say, well, you ask the questions. This is your show, not mine. Fact is, I still don't understand what you're doing hanging around this school and trailing after me. "Go ahead, ask your questions," is what she did say that first day. As I recall, my initial question had to do with how she got started in teaching.

"My mother taught school for years, so I decided I would follow her in the profession. Daddy always said she worked harder than he did. He was a factory foreman in Pittsburgh. They made automobile parts. I remember him saying things like how dedicated she was. That stuck with me. I remember, too, the pride she took in it, despite all of the difficulties they had then. It's amazing really, that that whole generation made it through as they did. They had so few black teachers in the city school systems at the time. They did have some, which is more than most people think. But God, they really had to fight it out for every inch."

"Your parents talk about it much?"

"No, not much." Her voice sounded wistful as her fingers touched her lips. "Very little actually. There were four of us, two boys and two girls. Another child died before I was born. They didn't have it easy. No one then had it easy, I suppose. Between your color and your money, you weren't about to go too far. Well, you know all this from studying sociology, right?" I nodded to her, hoping that she would say more. I often wonder what I communicated to her that made it so apparent that I felt vulnerable about the definition of my role with her. "I had an uncle killed in the Detroit race riot. You know about that?" she asked.

"Yes, I do."

"Good. Good for you. I'm teaching the history of it with my sixth-graders."

"School give you trouble about that?"

"No. Why should they?" She looked at me, her body very still.

"Well, I just thought . . ."

"You see," she interrupted me, her voice particularly calm, "that's the kind of question that's leading nowadays to the problem of this whole educational business. You ask a question hunting for some sort of racial tension. You see a black teacher who's doing something with her class, with young children especially, that has to do with race. Now, at once, two ideas go through your mind. First, you'd like to know how much of her curriculum is race. Right? Then, you look for a source of confrontation. Is the administration inhibiting her? Tension. Everyone's looking for tension. The thing that gets me is how you folks in social science or in graduate schools of education are promoting some of the same insidious ideas that radio and television do. One would think you would be more sensitive to what's happening. You always make it so glamorous . . ."

"The portrayal of slum schools is glamorous?" I had to interrupt her.

"Yes. It's glamorous. That's exactly what it is. Glamorous in the humanistic sense that, you know, great writers can make death look beautiful. There's no difference in your accounts of a really rotten school, or horrible conditions in a school, or the ghetto, or the slums. It's all romantic and glamorous; oppression is made glamorous. The lives of teachers are made glamorous . . ."

I became angry with her. True, she did not invite me to the school, but I had some right, I believed, to inquire about the school and the classes she taught.

"I think you have social science mixed up with television soap operas," I blurted out. She smiled at me for the first time.

"At least you got anger in you. That's one good step for you. Most of these reporters just take everything we hand out." She waited a moment studying me. "Anyway, you're right. I'm being too quick to mix the slop in with things that aren't quite as bad. But you folks really do dehumanize us even when you're not trying to. That's the part that makes me sick. You're a bit like tigers, curled up in low branches, waiting, waiting for something to walk by underneath you, so you can up and pounce on it."

"I don't think that's true, Miss Bottomly," I continued to argue. "I don't think that's always true. I really don't."

"Oh, don't go literal on me all of a sudden. You know what I'm talking about. Don't be so exact. And what the hell, if only one or two of you are snooping around hunting for a story, then that colors all of you. So it's one out of ten or twenty or a thousand. What's the difference for those of us who are getting snooped on? Either way, I have to stay on my guard every time I see a strange face."

"Like mine."

"Like yours. That's right. Like yours. I have to beware all the time. I'll tell you something; the big game has to do with just who really is whose ally around here. Teachers voting against one another or administrators making it tough. Isn't that what you hear?"

"Yes, I do." The status system of men and women, of high school and college teachers is changing, I was thinking then, four years ago when we had this conversation. But whether or not equality between the sexes or between teaching colleagues is actually being achieved, the feelings about equality or an ideology advancing equality are changing everywhere. Whatever the other person is thinking or saying during interviews like these, I have myriad thoughts running through my mind about wanting to invoke sex or class or position or maybe even race, so that I don't have to feel, well, what is the word? Threatened? Attacked? Put on the defensive? Perhaps it is just the uncomfortable irritability that comes from being interviewed. "I think I can confess to hearing some of that," I told her.

"Well," she said, letting out a long breath, "the real battle, you know, isn't always fought in school. I'm sad to admit that it isn't *always* the reactionary assistant principals who give us trouble. There are always teachers who line up along any side you'd like to see on any political position. But that isn't where the trouble lies. The problem is that the trouble lies in the nature of society. It lies across America. We're blanketed with it. I don't mind telling you, no matter what you decide to write, that it isn't an easy job working with nine-, ten-, eleven-, twelve-year-old children and making believe that we, all of us, aren't under that blanket of social disease and racism and the rich getting richer and the grammar school teacher going on and asking for a pay raise that would put us at the level of a butcher's assistant. We're all under that. Administrators too. You don't have to turn us against one another. The only people who suffer when you do that are the children, and my God they've had their share." She stopped speaking suddenly, as though listening to a playback of her own voice. "I sound so much like my mother. Here I'm giving you this speech, telling you things you know, I'm sure . . . well, I'm not sure. I'm not sure you or any of them have any feeling for what teaching is. What gets me more than anything is that all these articles and shows make it *impossible* for me to speak my piece. I have nothing to say anymore that is mine. My own, I mean. You do something good and it earns too much attention. The children in my class are even aware of that. They know when they do something and it earns more attention than they deserve.

"I'll tell you something else that bothers me. You take these books about the failure of education. Can you imagine the state of the art when you have people cleaning up because they've had bad experiences? Or been fired? What do you do if you can't write? What do you do if all you aspire to is a simple eight-to-three job working with children? That's all my training is for. *You* think there's something wrong with me if that's all I want out of life? You tell me!"

"No, I don't," I answered her. There is, however, a feeling I carry with me that I did speak about with Elaine. Not that first day but two years later, when we had become friends, and my own nervous push for equality had subsided, and her confidence in what I might eventually write had taken root. It is that I often envy the teachers she spoke about, the romantics as they are called, the martyrs. Despite the fact that I know that liberal-minded people like myself are especially fascinated with the deeds and misdeeds of these people, and that this fascination comes usually at times of crisis, and even then is part of a condescending attitude toward teachers, I envy them. Despite the many times, moreover, I have read and thought that no one speaks for anyone else, I crave to be one of the special ones who can, perhaps, speak for other human beings, public school teachers in this case, for Elaine Bottomly even, as if she could not speak for herself. As if in these pages she has not already spoken for herself.

"I'm not sure," she was continuing, "that these books do us more good or less good. I suppose I wish people would stop thinking that just 'cause you're working with children or living in the ghetto that you're so damned special. This country's got a thing for people being special. Everyone's going around seeking fame, grinding out the little they can from schools. Believe me, there aren't too many people going to get famous making a career in the public schools. I'm not certain about many things, but I am about that. Sometimes I think you all ought to make your political noises in the city hall and let the rest of us who just want to teach do our work. I swear, someday I'm going to lock up the door to my class, put a policeman outside, and tell him not to let a living soul come in."

"What would you do inside?" I wondered.

"I'd sit in a comfortable chair and read to the children." She paused, looking at me and shaking her head from side to side as though to correct herself. "On second thought," she grinned, "I'd put two policemen out there and double-lock the door and not tell anyone *what* I was doing with the children. Nobody's business what you do. I have credentials. People can visit when they want to. All the rest of the time though, I'd just as soon carry on alone."

"Lots of people would be unhappy with your stationing policemen outside your door," I smiled. I remember wanting to appear kind as I reached for some stale political ammunition. Elaine was infuriated by the remark.

"Let 'em. Let 'em all come in here and tell me about their radical politics and policemen in the school. I don't need people to tell me schools aren't a place for police. What do they think I am? Born yesterday? I'm tired of it, the rhetoric and the fads of politics. This year it's the community, maybe the schools, although I'm not so sure about that. You finally get a busing program going and between the white folks getting all up in arms about that and the media running around with their cameras, and you folks with your notebooks, you'd think this was Vietnam. Suppose you tell me, since you're always sniffing around schools, just where the politics tornado goes when I come to school every day? Huh? How come there aren't people ready to take over my job? How come we still need to work? How come *our* conditions are still so bad? They bus eight, ten kids from this school, and people like me, white and black, stay here and work with them. White folks too got to work with them. You got all these people shouting at us to throw the whites out of the school — where are they supposed to find work? And how do they know that some white teachers aren't doing one *helluva* good job? How do they know that?"

"Look, Miss Bottomly, all I was suggesting was that there are people out there . . ."

"Out where?"

"Outside of here, you know. C'mon. You know what I mean . . ."

"You mean people who aren't teaching?"

"Yes. Some of them. But teachers too who say that the police in schools only provoke the kids." I went on, my anger rising, and my inevitable need to make worthless political points not receding an inch. "And a lot of those say that white teachers ought to get out of black schools. That's what I'm saying. I mean, I don't want to start any fight with you. It isn't worth it."

"This isn't any fight. Now just relax. We're just feeling each other out. I'll tell you what I think. I'm one person talking. That's all. And that's the way they all should talk. I'm indignant. I don't need any folks coming here and telling me about the conditions of black children. They think I'm blind? They think I don't realize the pitiful abuse of these people? *My people!* They want me to listen to *them?* Then they have to work side by side with me, day in, day out! I can't use people coming in, making demands, and then disappearing. Two weeks later I see them pushing some other cause. They can't even remember where they met me. Nobody's worse than white folks who rule these schools and your city hall and this state and Washington. The whole white system. The day you can see your skin is black is the day you learn what white folks do to you. But when you get to be my age you realize that there are a lot of people out there, in here, everywhere, making it their business to run right over you, take what you have and leave nothing. Nothing! That's the kind of stuff I don't see in your articles. Where's all the patronizing I feel every day coming from? You think we make it up? You think I can just teach a class, walk in there in the morning, walk out in the afternoon? Every part of me causes problems for one person or another. It's my skin, my sex, my age, the fact that I'm richer than lots of white folks and black folks here. You wait for the confrontation or the crisis, but the day-by-day action doesn't ever seem to add up to anything to the press. Why don't you write an article about the fact that I walk around here, and in the eyes of one person or another I'm a snotty bitch or window dressing or an Oreo — you know what that is?"

"Yes, brown on the outside . . ." I started.

". . . white on the inside," she finished it for me. "An Oreo. Or a whore. A cheap black woman. That's what I contend with. I can't trust them, most of them, when they spend so much time talking with me. I can't be sure of them when they never talk to me. I have to make sure certain people will find out who I date; I have to make sure others don't know anything about my private life. Hah. That's a laugh. Private life. Where, I'd like to know? Lookit right here. I can tell what your politics are all about. You mouth what all the rest of them mouth. I tell you I see white men, that's going to offend you because you have this new notion of race. You have an idea that blacks have to stay together all the time. Every minute. Well, you can feel relieved. I live in Roxbury, so I'm not going to go out and mingle around in your neighborhoods."

"I think you're being unfair, Miss Bottomly. If you'd just as soon forget about me talking to you, that's all right."

"No. I never said anything about not talking. I just wanted to get the ground rules taken care of, because I know how you folks can distort what you hear. I'm just protecting myself."

"I guess I feel that that's too bad."

"Of course it's too bad," she said in response. "It's too bad education is in the state that it is. It's too bad that there's so much political stuff of a second-hand nature flying around here most of the time that you're too tired out from it all to have much energy left over for teaching. It's all too bad. It's too bad I can't follow the advice all my friends give me. Spill the beans on corrupt principals and racist teachers. It's all too bad."

"Why can't you?"

"You can't, I can't. It's your job to get some hot article, some inside angle on the schools. Me, I spill the beans, I don't have a job. That's why I can't. And your question shows just how far apart are our perspectives." We had finished eating and were walking back to her classroom. My first "official" interview would take place during the next thirty minutes while her class was at lunch and then recess. After our chat, the students would return and I would sit in the back observing. Miss Bottomly and I sat in little chairs. "This all right?" she inquired. I feigned exertion crouching on the child's seat, and she smiled. "I have some getting to be almost as big as you. They look just as funny."

"For some reason," I said, "you don't look uncomfortable or out of place in that chair."

"For many reasons," she replied. "I don't feel uncomfortable or out of place in here. I belong in here. I'm trained for this. I love this."

I admit to regularly entertaining an impulse to tell Elaine Bottomly that someday she should record her teaching experiences in a book, but I always remember her feelings about this before making any public suggestion. Moreover, as I go back over the notes of three and four years ago, I feel a second impulse. It is to tie together all that Elaine Bottomly said in that first visit, or perhaps take off from her words and develop some original concepts about the aspects of education that she encounters. I cannot rid myself of the need to make her somebody important, more important than she is, in her school, in her life outside, and to me. In response to this need, she herself has told me that "freedom is when you really, honest and truly let people decide their own fate and achieve the status they want. And then have a society that supports them in the decision they have made."

"Am I patronizing you by wanting more?" I asked her recently.

"No. Well, in a way. When we first met I'd have slapped your wrist if you'd said I should run for office or be a principal. Now I know you.

You're a strange man. It's like you want me and a lot of people really, to be, well, the word I get is immortal."

"I think that's probably right, Elaine. I'd like people to get their day in the sun."

"Yes, but don't you see that while that's nice and all that, it too is part of a brand of politics that can be awfully dangerous."

"Of course I do. I know about colonialization," I said.

"You don't need to keep impressing me with what you know about race issues. It's not even that complicated. Whatever it is, our parents, our own school days, the people we know, the times we just by fate happen to be born in, there are lots of people like me who don't aspire to more than what we have, or are just about to get. I remember our first visit. You were so damn eager. I told you that you didn't have much of an idea what was going on in schools like these. Remember?"

"Very well."

"'Member I told you that you never have to remind a black person about what's happening to him in America?"

"Yes," I replied.

"It still holds. I'll never be rid of the feeling of strangeness, you know, the odd one in a company of whites, and the relief of being in a room with just my brothers and sisters. That's never ever going to change. Even if I were blind, my ears would tell me where they are." Her tone was even and peaceful. "But that doesn't mean I want more than what I have. I'll continue reading the experts. Like you." She grinned. "All you writing types, but don't make wishes for me. Maybe the next one will be won over by your wishes. I'm not. Do I want more money? You better believe it, honey. Do I want freedom in this school and a chance to really let out and try experiments with the children, knowing that some simply have to fail? You know I do. Would I like America to change, I mean really do an about-face? I'd take it in a minute. But that's all different, I think, from what you want for me. I really think so."

"I'm not sure, Elaine," I offered. "I'm not sure."

"Well, then I may be wrong, but you haven't convinced me yet. Not yet."

"I'm not sure," is all I could tell her.

"C'mon, let's see what you wrote from that first visit. I want to see whether I can recognize myself. 'Member what I told you about recognizing yourself? You white folks, you really get me, you know that?" She looked first at me, then at the pile of notes I had amassed from our first day together. By the end of the second page she knew that I had not forgotten the conversation that had preceded what was to be the first of our official interviews. She looked up proudly, and I felt that I might have been one of her sixth-graders, indeed one who had just done rather well in his project for the year.

"You dirty dog," she said smiling. "You dirty, dirty dog."

chapter twelve

the
chicanos'
run
to
freedom

schools, communities,
and social change

the setting for this chapter is Alamosa, a town located in the southern part of Colorado. The purpose of my trip there was to visit Adams State College and to learn more of the Chicano movement for freedom. No doubt, education is a vital part of this movement, for the full inclusion of any minority group members in a society often begins with their admission to schools which historically have excluded them. More generally, politics and social change find a logical although vulnerable arena in educational institutions.

There are some who allege that school is precisely where social protest movements should commence and be nurtured. Others disagree. Though acknowledging education's role in social change and patterns of social and occupational mobility, they insist that schools strive for academic excellence and not let social and political movements interfere with this goal. To some, the Chicanos' appeal is felt to be unoriginal or derivative since it follows on the heels of the Black Movement. Others see it as a splintered movement in which various political positions are assumed. These facts complicate not only the task of the young Chicanos described in chapter twelve, but their relationships with their fellow students, teachers, and community members as well.

Most schools cannot hide from their political associations and beliefs, as much as they might like to appear free of them. Students experience the political implications of education, as well as the effect that they themselves have on their schools in light of their changing attitudes about politics. It is not uncommon, as we know, for people of all ages to shift their political positions, or to alter the intensity of their feeling about these positions. In both its formal and informal ways, education influences these shifts even if this is not one of its stated purposes. Accordingly, some people contend that they are being brainwashed by their teachers or colleagues, whereas others insist that school neutralizes or derogates their political goals. Some make us see educational oppression; others demand that we not forget America's pluralistic nature and the range of its political spectrum.

Political goals, like educational goals, are pursued ostensibly for the purpose of improving the conditions of human lives. When these goals conflict, the tension in societies, communities, and schools rises to the point of explosion. After the explosion, should it come, those who remain must determine whether or not their lives have been enhanced, and their rights and culture safeguarded.

Because of the fact that our study in this chapter focuses as much on a school and a community as it does on any particular person, actual names and places have been retained. Special permission was granted by those whose words are included in the chapter.

Six of us sat down to dinner in the restaurant. Having selected a table in one of the building's wings, we were ushered instead to a table near the curved bar. A Kiwanis meeting would occupy the space we had chosen, and anyway the second-choice table was located right under the little video-jukebox machine. So the six of us, three Chicanos, two Anglos, and a black, prepared for dinner. Michael, one of the young Chicanos, laughingly talked about cowboys he had seen dining in this very restaurant. He pronounced the word ca-*boys*. Sure enough, several men entered the restaurant wearing the familiar boots. They walked as though they might well have been cowboys. After a long wait our orders were taken. We requested beer with our meat and fish. "Don't order Coors," Ronald Gallegos advised us. "Those people are hurting the Chicanos." Moments later we were asked to show proof of our ages. We were perturbed, although it is a bit encouraging to be seen as young. The waitress, however, was angered.

Outside the sun was setting over the San Luis Valley in southern Colorado. Only the tops of the foothills shone with daylight. Soon it would be cool again, and if there were people living up in the caves notched in the hills they would shiver through the night and pray that tomorrow's warm sun might comfort them before the painful chills made their lives even more unbearable. Migrant workers living, hiding in the caves above Alamosa, Colorado, population 8,000, parceling out an amount of food so small that their children and their elders will die, here, in New Mexico, in Indiana and Florida and Texas too, of starvation.

Inside, the six of us speak of the Movement, of La Raza, and of Corky Gonzales' work in Denver. We speak of pure revolution, whatever that might mean, of the future of Chicano people, and of promises to ship lobsters from Boston to my new friends in Colorado. The name of Chavez is mentioned several times, and produce like grapes, cantaloupes, and lettuce is mentioned with an unusual reverence. "You know about Tijerina?" I am asked. I do. "Trujillo?" No. "Ché you obviously know. Who doesn't?"

"Are there many Indians around here?" I inquire. A few. They stay by themselves. Then the three Chicanos speak of their Indian heritage. All claim Indian blood. Arnold Gallegos recalls his grandparents. The others, too, remember Indian traditions, the dances and ceremonial warpaint, a special character of human behavior, and the faces of Indians. Ron knows his family to be descended from Aztecs, although for generations his family has lived in the Valley, a valley that the local college announces in its catalogue to be larger than the state of Connecticut.

Suddenly, music starts in both wings of the restaurant. Before convening, the Kiwanis group is singing "God Bless America." Simultaneously, an unearthly counterpoint stabs me behind the right ear. The video-jukebox is alive. Vibrating rock sounds that remind me of strip shows in Boston and Chicago are revving up, and, snap, the little television screen lights up revealing a white woman, that is, an Anglo, who dances about, thinly clad, as they say in the paperback novels, grinding and bumping her way through some erotic bedtime ablutions. It is all utterly preposterous. The music, the medium, the ridiculous gyrations and images of the woman. My neck aches from watching.

When she stops, we resume talking. The Chicanos razz me. The one woman with us smiles shyly. She is very quiet. "What have you learned at the college?" they want to know. "Who did you speak to?" Did you see the President?" "What's happening there?" For the moment it seems as though they cannot trust the impressions they themselves have shared earlier that day at the College Information Center on Bell Avenue, Centro-Emiliano-Zapata de Aztlan. Maybe they wish us, my friend and me, to affirm and make legitimate their claims, their despair even, and, of course, the Movement. Perhaps they fear the tension between their word and the word of the men administering the College with which they deal. But we cannot continue, for again rhythmic cues are heard above us and the bawdy television show reappears. I assume it will be the same as before, but it isn't. For now a black woman performs her equally erotic, equally ludicrous bathroom and bedroom choreography. She seems to be looking for directions from an unseen person, and as she flops around on the bed I think of the billions of American stimuli that each of us sucks in every day of our plastic and organic lives.

Together we watch the woman. She is nude. No flimsy apparel this time. I lean across the table to my friend and mutter something about racism. The Chicanos don't understand at first. "What did he say?" "Where's the racism?" We explain: white clothed, black stripped. "Yes, yes. That's right." "That's good," they respond.

Education, the special programs, the origin and purpose of Adams State College in Alamosa, the percentages quoted in books and brochures having to do with Chicanos in this particular region and in this one school, numbers and words which have filled our heads are for the moment meaningless. A naked black woman who does indeed look frightened and maybe even ashamed dances in the mechanical lights above our heads. The waitress brings sherbet in pewter cups and angrily plops them down in the middle of our plates. Potatoes, steak, sour cream, gravy, bubble onto the table. We look at one another. The black woman's diffidence and nudity blink off. The Kiwanis men laugh after taking a vote on something. People in the booths stare at us. We fish sherbet bowls out of the plates.

"What do you think of the Movement?" Michael has asked. I talk on about despising the fact that revolutions and movements are even necessary. It just shouldn't be, I dream. What I tell him is all foolish; it is from my heart and all, but simpleminded and utterly uncomplicated. "Are we revolutionaries?" he asks me.

"No, I don't think so," I respond unthinkingly. Death, killing, explosives, I realize, have come to form my criteria, my mementos of revolution. And thus I have not honored him at all.

The dinner scene is almost concluded. As arranged, I pay for myself and my friend. Our combined bill totals a little under nine dollars. I give the waitress ten dollars. "Don't leave a tip," Michael orders me.

"Aren't you?" I ask, as though we could possibly condone this scene of antipathy and rejection.

"Hell no, man," he comes back. "This is what I take every day of my life. I don't pay extra for it. Besides," he begins to smile, "I don't have any more money." We laugh together. The Kiwanis group has adjourned. The people at the bar behind us sip their drinks. In the kitchen Chicanos wash dishes and clean up. None of them enters the front of the restaurant. I shall not see the waitress again, nor will I receive my change.

In the street, facing the Municipal Building, not far from Main Street, we meet more friends. Then all of us trudge upstairs to observe a City Council Meeting. A half-dozen men or so, seated around tables pushed together to form a T, discuss property values and a request from someone to purchase a dilapidated house not far from the barrio. The Chicanos are waiting for permission to march and celebrate a holiday in a park which they soon will rename Zapata Park. Permission, however, has been granted before our arrival, and so we walk to Arnie's house where some children are rehearsing their dances for the coming celebration.

The Chicanos' Run to Freedom   209

On the way to Arnie's, Michael and I see two young women seated on the concrete doorstep of a Main Street hotel, a block or two from the Rialto movie theater. Along the street, boys and girls are seated on parked cars, talking together and waving and whistling to the traffic. It could be the 1940's, wartime perhaps. Wartime, when hometown fun means sitting around or watching a parade. We engage the women in conversation. One looks Mexican, the other not at all. Both are Chicanas. They are passing time awaiting the opening of Adams State's fall term. I ask questions of them, a journalist to the end. Michael cannot take the slow pace.

"What do you think of the Movement?" he asks harshly. They are surprised.

One responds: "You mean the Chicanos?"

"Of course," he snaps back.

"Are you for them or against them?" she asks.

"Are you serious, man?" he responds. Neither woman wants any part of politics. They seek an education, nothing else. The night, its secrets, its possible adventures overcome them. They are Chicanas, but not at all eager to enter any fight or organized movement.

"You mean it's all right to get pushed around, to have men working in the fields for practically nothing?" Michael prods them. They still want no part of it. "Have you ever gotten thrown out of a bar?" They nod, yes. "And that doesn't bother you?"

"Not really," is the answer. "Once," the Mexican-looking woman says, "they pulled out the cord of the jukebox when my boyfriend played our music." Michael is on fire.

"That's it. That's it," he says. She admits she was mad, but still it is not enough to make her join a movement or be for anyone or against anyone. We leave them on the steps.

At Arnie's house, young children rehearse the ritual steps of their dance. Two women instruct them under the dull lights in the garage. A group of us stand together at the door watching boys unself-consciously learn to skip on one foot as the other foot crosses in front later to take their slight weight, all with a rhythm and form that a culture has traced for them. We beam with pride as though they were our children. On the back steps, several adults speak quietly together in the darkness. Music plays in the garage and the black outlines of the mountains above Alamosa loom up above the roofs. I have been absorbed into a tradition, a history of Americans, people quarreling among themselves about their very name: Mexican-Americans, Spanish, Spanish-speaking, Spanish-surname, Americans, Chicanos. The very word *Chicano*, its masculine form filled with power and strength, sexuality, persistence, and militancy, is the name I find congenial. Within minutes of my meeting with Arnold Gallegos and his family, I am comfortable with a new handshake. They grip my hand, as is the accustomed way, and then, as I lower it, we clasp one another's thumb, and then again the whole hand. It is a special enduring connection, a linking of human contact that means brother, compatriot, fellowman. On the campus of Adams State College, which now awaits the arrival of the remainder of its students, the football players having been at work for several days, I shall not feel this handshake even once.

Most of us know a bit about the Chicano movement, some of the statistics and some of the better-known political leaders and writers. We are aware of the Chicano programs going on at well-known colleges in El Paso, Santa Barbara, Santa Cruz, or we can imagine what they would be like, and we are aware of the student demonstrations and labor protests that have occurred in larger cities where the Chicano population is a small minority indeed. What we tend to know less about, however, are the places in the Southwest where Anglo institutions of higher education stand in the midst of towns where, numerically, Mexican-Americans are the majority. Adams State College, located in Alamosa, Colorado, some two hundred and twenty miles south and west of Denver, is one of these institutions. Every day its students, faculty, and administration feel the impress of demands and hopes, collective movements and individual passions, each of which would drive the college in a different direction, and each of which is supported by the invoking of a law or statistic that should forever make that desired direction absolute. For some in the college, the demands of community leaders and certain students must be pushed aside for the moment, as the needs of higher education — honoring credentials, developing legitimate curricula, and securing a national reputation — require constant attention. For others, the voices of Chicanos throughout America arouse feelings they had long ago thought might never be reawakened, feelings that most certainly had no place in college when they were students. And then suddenly, the feelings, the anger, the pride, and the hurt are back again, only this time they are painted over with political rhetoric and the inevitable statistics of injustice. The one statistic that reverberates in every room where Chicanos gather in this college is that at least 50 percent of the San Luis Valley, in which Alamosa is located, is Mexican-American, whereas Adams State reports less than 16 percent Mexican-Americans in its student body. It is a statistic that symbolizes, perhaps, the tension that colleges concerned with Mexican-Americans live with every day.

Generally, the presence of Mexican-American students on college campuses like Adams State — the presence, that is, of Spanish, of Chicano students, for the name we select reveals the portion of a heritage and the brand of purpose we, the present innkeepers of colleges, wish to honor — is a presence that not many institutions know well. In *Minority Access to College*, Fred E. Crossland reports that 2.4 percent or five million people in this country were, in 1970, Mexican-Americans. A report prepared by a committee of the American Political Science Association listed the number of Mexican-Americans at eight million. Of the total enrollment in higher education, 0.6 percent were Mexican-American, a percentage slightly lower than the percentage of Mexican-American college freshmen in 1970. The statistics of presence become even more dramatic in California, where, according to Harry Kitano and Dorothy Miller (in *An Assessment of Educational Opportunity Programs in California Higher Education*), blacks and Chicanos represent 18.3 percent of the state's population. Yet, they represent only 3.8 percent of the university, 11 percent of the community college, and 5.8 percent of the state college populations. The statistics, naturally, are often inaccurate, for we know well about census taking and minority groups. In "College and University Business," for example, Gilbert J. Chavez, Director of Spanish-Speaking Affairs in the Washington Office of Education, quotes these same California percentages in terms of Spanish surnames, a rather misleading, though indicative, guideline.

Not long ago, Mexicans, as Ernesto Galarza refers to them (in "Institutional Deviancy: The Mexican-American Experience"), were essentially a rural people living in the Southwest and working primarily as field hands. Urbanization and industrialization have now brought about a situation in which perhaps 95 percent of Mexican-Americans live in cities like Los Angeles, Denver, San Jose, and Phoenix. Their history, our history, has been shrouded with vile circumstances — the lasting pains of having been conquered in a war, and a patron system which exists today under the aegis of state and federal laws that should have done away with its destructive charters years ago. The history contains the treatment by the Catholic Church, its beneficence and the arrival of a caring ministry, as well as its self-aggrandizement, its long lists of oversights, and forms of oppression. The Church, among so many institutions, has at times cast a light upon the Mexican-American family such that grandparents, parents, and children were brought closer together through a belief in a loving God, but also through a contention that English must be the sole language, and the United States the sole source of culture and the single thread of an achieved destiny. In some families it is the shadow of the Church, the rise of black militancy, and the growing, though bumpy, development of a national student movement that cut into what Galarza calls the Mexican community's "extenuated family," causing young students to bolt from their families, causing sons to plead with their fathers to quit the fields and forsake the sense of beholden duty that binds them, like oxen, to the Anglo's plow.

No doubt, the ideal pluralism of America is the actual pluralism of any minority group. The distinctions between the rural and urban, between the Catholic- and public-school educated, and between those who live in the barrios and those who now call the established communities of Denver and Los Angeles or the fraternity houses on certain campuses their home, cause bitter tensions among this group of Americans. No doubt, too, education rests near or at the center of the most conflictive, yet crucial portion of a single human being as he or she embraces and absorbs, resists or cowers under the bits of culture, style, and behavior that history and society lay out. For minority people, much of education becomes the constant bombardment of socialization, acculturation, and assimilation patterns. And if these words sound too much like introductory sociology, then let us say it is contamination, as a handsome Indian woman in Boulder called it, that people must fear. Some Americans have chosen to call themselves Chicanos so that they might stand out not only in a culture they understand as well as any of us, but in a context of their own heritage, their own families, indeed the very people who wince at the sound of what they hear as a lower-class, revulsive, and overly political term. "That the minority communities are different," Rene Nuñez writes in *The Minority Student on Campus,* "is obvious in the fact that we have resisted acculturation to the point of dropping out of your schools and your society at a record-breaking pace" (pp. 130–131). Jesús Chavarría writes in the same volume: "I would say that this country has long perpetuated the myth that it is a pluralistic society. It is not. In this country, you either assimilate into the dominant culture, or else the dominant institutions, and that includes educational institutions, are irrelevant to you."

Chicano. It is a most complicated stimulus to many people. For some it rings with *machismo,* power, hope, and they run to it as a source of life. For others, the word brings a smile, they shake their heads in bewilderment, for they think of an identification with Mexicans, and what it might mean to have soul or die in the street for a dream. Chicano. How long will it be, some ask with their eyes, before the media, the writers, and the educators neutralize this term, this one simple word from which the electricity of revolution might some day be generated. And for others, it is a term to be kept out of sight, a symbol of a culture's history in which one simply cannot find pride or a positive lesson. It is a part of a child's body that some would keep covered, even in sleep. For these people, the threat of being called a sellout or coconut — brown on the outside, white on the inside — an Uncle Tomahawk, as the Indians would say, cannot affect their ideals and immediate aims.

Everyone who reads or watches television or listens to the talk in the subways and buses can guess what the Chicano might want. In large cities like Denver, where Corky Gonzalez's Crusade for Freedom has recently pushed itself up against the white form that powers the city, it is not surprising to hear calls for the firing of a police chief, for employment conditions to improve, for health care, housing, and educational opportunities to be directed to Chicanos, and for a voice in the decisions that are termed political but that have to do with fundamental human existence. In some places, as in New Mexico, if the Chicano Movement has not been efficacious, then at least Mexican-Americans occupy some positions of power and thereby have limited access to a cherished mobility. In Arizona, due perhaps to migration and settlement patterns, the going has been more difficult. Chicanos are lost in the crowds of conservative government and a righteous honoring of a history that should have come to an end with the last century. The Governor of Arizona proclaims a John Birch Day; but the demands that more Chicano instructors be employed at all educational levels, that culture-free tests be instituted for placement and as measures of human propensity, and that money be made available for minority children fall not on deaf ears exactly, but on ears ringing with the noises of power, elitism, accommodation, and, always, denial and safety. And how can it be that a visitor to San Antonio, Texas, would, in two weeks time, see no Mexican faces? Surely they are there, hidden somewhere in the county, working their way through jobs as sacrificial victims, perhaps, so that a generation down the line might be made visible.

It sounds utterly familiar, a series of images, formulas, and pleas that reach us whites, us Anglos, so regularly we can even afford to criticize the Chicano Movement now and then for being derivative and lacking an authentic basis. How many times have we heard those figures, those configurations of minority group anguish and inchoate political arousal? The Irish, the Italians, the Poles, the blacks, and now the Chicanos have made their move. One can feel their movement, their crush on the present, their leaning on the moments of education, and their thoughtful and poised contemplations for thirty years hence. Many young Chicanos feel with a severe intensity the words written about them by Chavarría: ". . . if he goes through school, if he makes it, he is bastardized. He becomes a Mexican-American — a man who is not; a man who is not Mexican, who is not American; a man who hangs limply between two cultures; a man who dangles. Why does he experience this? Because he is denied his language." But many young Chicanos feel, too, that their cause is less real because it comes upon the heels of the blacks. Like workers in a food line, they watch the few blacks in their communities receive their political allowance and educational dole first, while they wait their turn. (One school, I was informed recently, populated with 12 percent Indian students, inaugurated a black studies program in keeping with the educational swells of the East and West coasts. At the time of this inauguration, the school listed one black student in its records. Fifty more were promptly found. An Indian studies program had not yet been planned.)

All of this comprises the background against which one examines the presence of Chicanos in a school like Adams State. Founded in 1921 as the State Normal School at Alamosa by Colorado's General Assembly, the school's name was changed in 1929 to honor W. H. (Billy) Adams, a man from the Valley who became state senator and later, governor. By 1945 the teachers college label was removed, and the school presently functions as a major liberal arts college with special emphasis in education. At the time of Senator Adams, quite a few people believed that at least this one state school would care for the people of the community. From its inception, Adams State, under the leadership of President Richardson, forbade the establishment of fraternities and sororities because of discriminatory clauses in their national charters. Several years ago a student elected to the school's Associated Students and Faculty (A.S. & F.), one of the few such forms of academic government that survives, supported the introduction of fraternities and sororities, but a campus referendum voted him down four to one. Adams State keeps its doors open to everyone. All the various deans remain especially sensitive to the importance not only of admitting students but of guiding them all the way to graduation. The travesty of the revolving door junior college procedures will not come to pass at Adams State, which can now boast the fifth largest number of Mexican-American graduates.

Approximately three thousand students were enrolled at Adams State in 1970, with slightly more men than women in attendance. Almost three hundred of these were graduate students working on master's degrees or in the area of educational specialist, a unique six-year program terminating somewhere between a master's and doctorate level. About twelve hundred students reside on campus. (Those who commute may live as far as thirty or forty miles from Alamosa.) Approximately 37 percent of students receive some form of financial aid. About 50 percent of the Mexican-American students receive this aid, an amount averaging $749.63. The average amount for black students is slightly higher ($836.18). The average for all students is $562.30. A rough estimate of yearly expenses comes to $1,700. According to Financial Dean Melvin Clark, almost everybody who needs some assistance will in fact receive it, although first priority goes to in-state students and upperclassmen. In all, Dean Clark oversees about two hundred thousand dollars in scholarship monies, but with campus employment and federal and state work study programs included his budget totals nearly one million dollars. (The actual amount paid to athletes in the form of compensation for services rendered was never disclosed.) In the past, a sizeable amount of money came in the form of a state appropriation for minority students pursuing teaching degrees. With the present surplus of teachers, however, this fund will soon be phased out. And so the question for this former military officer is, "Just exactly how much do these people need?"

To many, Adams State is seen as the home of the Chicanos. For a long while El Parnaso, a sort of cultural affairs student group, kept alive the mood and culture of the Mexican-American students, and, in arranging for dances and exhibits, brought gratification and an ambience of amicable coexistence to the school. Now, a second organization has been developed. United Mexican-American Students (UMAS) has taken on a more political role. It is UMAS that pushes for increased numbers of Chicano students and Chicano faculty. (Presently, about 14 percent of the faculty is Mexican-American and most of these people are graduates of Adams State.) It is UMAS that works with Arnold Gallegos, the director of the Talent Search Program in the barrio, and with tutoring programs aimed at helping students on campus, as well as those still in high schools and grade schools. The members of UMAS seem somewhat less than ecstatic about the Hispanic Studies curriculum which Adams State has long offered. They seek political representation, jobs for Chicanos, an honoring of the Spanish language, and, as the deans suggest, visibility. The school itself has taken part in working with local business groups and the chamber of commerce to increase the number of available jobs. A ski jacket factory and a potato processing firm were developed with assistance from the college. College personnel frequently sit with Chicano leaders in meetings or during community celebrations. But always there is the problem of money. The alumni are attempting to raise grant money. The legislature helps a bit. An Upward Bound program that would have made a difference was rejected by Washington. A man on the faculty has recently been appointed to work solely on the problem of raising money and enhancing Chicano programs, but this does not satisfy the local Chicanos who continue to argue that they have meager representation in the school, although they have manageable working relationships with several of its important officers.

In reflecting upon UMAS, Dean John Turano said: "I'm happy with the prospect of them being aggressive. They can do a lot for the Valley and for Colorado, and contribute to our national purposes. We have the job of accommodating pluralism. If we don't, we'll tear ourselves apart. The idiosyncrasies of the Spanish must be looked at objectively. We must see the good things in these people and not try to change them. Let's not stop cooking tacos or spaghetti and see how it all fits in." Holding to this philosophy, Turano nonetheless points to the competition between Spanish-speaking groups. Regularly he is called in to deal with Mexican-Americans in the community who question the plans and programs of students and faculty, and the effect on the school of proverbial outside agitators.

President John A. Marvel, the college's fifth president, is quick to report the problems of a liberal Anglo college in a Mexican-American conservative community. He tells of his care for the Spanish people and, like all those one interviews at Adams State, he elucidates the connotations of that one scintillating word: Chicano. While only 2 percent of the school's population is black (some sixty-five students mainly from Denver and Colorado Springs), their own wave of protest and demand preceded that of the Spanish by some two years. Perhaps the Chicanos took their cue from the blacks, but if they did, according to Dr. Marvel, they have been unable to organize with the same integrity and smoothness blacks seem able to sustain. Nonetheless, the college's administration "must make them responsible, visible, and give them credence." One problem, Dr. Marvel suggests, is that the students cannot get as close to faculty members as they can to some administrators. And still, as is true everywhere, many people just hope "the problem" will go away.

Wishing to learn about student motivation and that special quest of minority youth for visibility and for signs of mainstream middle-American success, Dr. Marvel helped institute a summer seminar program for his administrative staff. He requested Professor Paul A. Delgado, a sociologist, to prepare a report on the "Minority Students at Adams State." On page 2 of the Delgado report, four features of social movements described originally by sociologists Leonard Broom and Phillip Selznick were outlined as a basis on which to understand the Chicano Movement. They included: "a distinctive perspective and ideology"; "a strong sense of solidarity and idealism"; "an orientation to-

ward action"; and the statement, "A movement is usually made up of a variety of forms and groupings." In his copy, in the margin alongside this paragraph, Dr. Marvel had written: "Can these be reconciled in an Anglo-oriented institution?"

In addition to the Delgado report, Dr. Marvel rounded up and printed a list of thirteen "Minority Appeals and Institutional Responses." They included: "1. There should be greater emphasis on Hispanic Studies. 2. Efforts should be made to provide sensitivity or 'rap' sessions for the administrators, faculty, students, and community leaders on minority student problems and aspirations. 3. El Parnaso dances and cultural events need more exposure. . . . 7. The defensible political objectives of UMAS should be perpetuated. . . . 10. We should magnify our similarities more than our differences between the races. . . ." Later the President added to the list: "14. The Ombudsman program [and] 15. Human Dignity Committee." (Nothing is said here about funds or scholarships. Nor is anything mentioned about obtaining money for scholarships in the President's report, at least not in the section devoted to efforts for the future. In this particular document, many important new plans are announced involving the expansion of present academic programs and counseling services, the establishment of new career education programs and teacher-student advisory committees, and the relocation of the football field and track.)

Dr. Marvel cannot easily reconcile the hundreds of orientations, perspectives, and hopes driven by passion and even rage extant on his campus. He appreciates full well the need to increase communication between sectors of his academic community in which he has blacks wanting black faculty, Chicanos wanting more of their kind everywhere — support for their groups like MECHA (*Movimiento Estudiantil Chicano de Aztlan*), and for Chicano programs not unlike those at Santa Barbara where Chavarría teaches, Fresno State, San Diego State, or El Paso — and students of all backgrounds wanting jobs both during college years and afterwards. He has developed forums and special groups like an Awareness Committee attempting to detect and resolve problems, and a complicated organizational chart in which program chairmen, deans, and directors along with a Faculty Advisory Council and a Council for Improvement of Teaching and Learning are interspersed in the power hierarchy of the college.

President Marvel also faces the problem of an inevitable Anglo backlash, for some now contend that Chicanos ask for and are awarded too much. Noises of this backlash arose over the question of money allocated to athletes and athletic programs. Early in the year, Chicanos argued that athletes receive an excessive amount of money in light of what is needed to put students through school. Football coach Ronald T. Harms has no concern about race, naturally, when he picks his starting lineups. But when he announces that he has young men on his preseason squad from Hoboken to Los Angeles, one suspects that not too many Chicanos from the Valley, or from Arizona or New Mexico for that matter, will survive the final cuts.

The backlash emerged in the midst of A.S. & F. elections when UMAS ran an entire minority slate. In the past, Chicano students had won homecoming and sweetheart queens, but their representation in college government had been minimal at best. It was a significant election with 60 to 70 percent of the students and faculty voting. But as in all elections, the stories of chicanery abounded in this valley college. Some said that members of the athletic department handed out the names of candidates whom their students were to vote for if they were to retain their scholarships. The athletic department repudiates this story: "There is nothing to the fact that any member of the physical education department told students who to vote for."

The minority slate, at least the Chicanos on it, lost by less than ten votes. Two of the slate's blacks were victorious. Forty votes, however, went unaccounted for. "It was all muffed," lamented Leroy Payne, a senior who later, admittedly, would be ramrodded into A.S. & F. where he now sits as the lone Chicano on the council. Deeply upset, some students complained to President Marvel about the elections. They even visited a Rural Legal Service, desperately seeking recourse. But in time, as always happens, the energy drains, the spirit subsides, and those who seek a magical reduction of danger are, in their way, rewarded. From Dr. Marvel's perspective, the athletic affair is illegitimate since students themselves vote on the amount of money this one department receives in the form of athletic fees. It is, in a word, "a scapegoat." Indeed, he upheld the students' decision to reduce the athletic budget by $8,000 last year. Thirty-eight men presently hold football scholarships, and to

slice it lower than this would be to make it impossible for a coaching staff to field an adequate team, much less one that could make it to the top of its conference. On the other side of the campus, Coach Harms supports campus political action and denies the existence of a backlash. To be sure, many athletes joined the group opposing the Chicano slate, but only because they feared the presence of a united and organized minority group as much as they feared a change in the balance of power.

Before I left his office, Dr. Marvel spoke of equity in financial distribution and minority representation on forty campus committees. Mexican-Americans are often provided with college office jobs, just as they may be awarded positions in the seven international study centers with which Adams State is affiliated, the first having been established in Mexico. Adams State students may now spend an academic year in Montreal, Rome, Copenhagen, India, Singapore, East Africa, and Brazil. It is an adventurous and romantic program, but how strange the ring of that phrase, "a junior year abroad," here in Alamosa where for many Americans a trip to Pueblo or Mesa Verde is a colossal dream.

In the first floor offices of the main administration building I spoke with a few Mexican-Americans who work for the college and who said, almost before I asked, that they have always been shown a fair deal: no discrimination on campus, no shortchanging. A young woman was frightened by my questions as I pushed too hard to unearth the problems of the community. A graduate of Adams State, she will soon become an elementary school teacher, probably in a small town if a job arises. She might like to leave the Valley for a while, but big cities seem overwhelming and frightening. Militancy and crime are enough to keep her in the country towns. Chicano studies, she reported, seem unimportant at this time. "We are, after all, Americans, and so it is important for us to learn American history." She has observed Anglos and Spanish "getting along," but the blacks appear to her to be interacting with no one but themselves. Just before we separated she told me of her father, a janitor possessing a talent for welding. They resent his color where he works, she said, and although he has passed a test of some sort, he remains unable to find a job in which his talent might be honored.

A young man in the same office recounted a similar story. Sam Ortiz, another graduate of Adams State, complained of the advantage taken by certain Spanish people and the decent, generous programs that too many abuse. The son of a mine employee and machinery painter, Sam and his brothers are now "doing well." His sisters never attended college. All the children went to Catholic school where his own children, Timothy and Samantha, also will go, for the education is good there and the personal attention and unwavering discipline essential for proper human development. Sam Ortiz knows the social history and the problems of his people and his college as well as anyone else. He sees the Spanish people of the state as the homesteaders, and now, having married an Anglo, he has experienced from all sides the friction between groups. He worries about what he calls the invasion and take-over by "colored people from the East." But if this is deplorable to him, so too is UMAS and other political interest groups who crave handouts merely because they have been discriminated against for so long. "It burns me up that I work, that I had two jobs. My parents didn't give us a penny. No one ever gave us anything. If you want something bad enough you can get it. Lots of people just don't want to hustle." Then, after sitting in silence for a moment, he confessed that perhaps he is angry because few of today's programs, procedures, and styles of momentum existed when he was a student. Not a draft dodger, he assures me, he is willing to pay taxes like all other responsible citizens. And if he is seen by some as a sell-out? "I don't live for my race or my religion. I live for my children — for my parents and brothers and sisters. I could care less about anyone else. I won't put my job in jeopardy."

Whatever the vicissitudes of Sam Ortiz's life, a man like Professor Lawrence Gomez, who administers Teacher Corps at Adam State, regards the scene from a slightly different perspective. For Professor Gomez, the telling statistics relate to the percentage of Anglo and Mexican-American students who graduate from high school but never attend college, despite the fact that tests indicate they could handle the work. Teacher Corps, like Alamosa's Migrant Council, is associated with Adams State essentially through UMAS. Assuming a self-professed radical position, Teacher Corps' goals are to strengthen educational opportunities and to encourage institutions of higher education to broaden all educational programs. Five school districts presently are served by a program that attempts to work with the specific learning needs of a particular population. Teacher Corps will be examining demonstrable skills and competencies rather than evaluating students according to traditional criteria.

For Larry Gomez, discrimination is a daily experience. It was this way in high school and at Adams State as well. For eighteen years, his father-in-law has worked for a local farmer seventy to eighty hours a week. Just recently the man has raised his valued employee's salary from $75 to $90 per month. But one does not so easily convince a talented designer such as this father-in-law to give up the ways of the patron system. Nor does one easily eradicate the shame of the two boys who, moments ago laughing together on the sidewalk, now reveal embarrassment because they cannot speak English well enough to direct a visitor to the post office. But still, Professor Gomez sighs, some in his own family direct their children to learn only English. In the Teacher Corps program, however, Spanish will be honored along with all other facets of the Chicano culture. Indeed, the words *Chicano* and *Chicana* will be spoken regularly, even though their mere sound will not ease the brittle relationships between Teacher Corps and UMAS on the one hand, and certain administrators and faculty on the other.

Ironically, the words, the languages really, are precisely what some faculty would see as representing one of the most severe problems experienced by Mexican-American students. The Spanish of the Valley, Professor Louis D. Appel noted, is an "inferior regional dialect" nowhere near as eloquent as the "universally accepted" language spoken in Spain. Students enter college, therefore, deficient in both English *and* Spanish, a fact, Professor Appel reported, that makes the Mexican-American self-conscious and pessimistic about his chances. Regrettably, many faculty do little to encourage him. Yet, while some faculty members would stand totally behind the Chicano Movement, others react to the inevitable question about students' demands for an increased number of Chicanos by warning that "no college can have a raison d'être if it builds its policies on ethnic quotas. . . . One cannot hire faculty merely because of their backgrounds, for a lack of competency would prove disadvantageous to the students themselves. Doors must remain open to all students," Professor Appel stated, but in readjusting ethnic proportions, "one cannot advocate the firing of an Anglo merely to increase the percentage of Chicanos. The ethnic experience of another can only be known vicariously, but ethnicity or race cannot ever supplant or compensate for knowledge. If we can recruit Chicano or black scholars, Godspeed. . . . But our society remains 90 percent white and there must be some gratification on the part of blacks, for example, that whites would want to teach black literature." Like the Negro culture, Professor Appel concluded, the Spanish culture is impoverished.

It is of course easy to be an educational journalist and travel thousands of miles to a college in a portion of the country one hardly recognizes as his own, and day by day hear in the streets a language one knows for sure is not his own, and then witness, in simple relief, the skirmish lines of various educational constituents. Self-interest, institutional maintenance, cross-pressures, and financial hierarchies, all the warhorses of higher education are extant in this one college community. For education, as we know, is an arena of social change, maybe even of revolution, just as it remains what it has always been, a corridor of mobility and advancement. But a most impressive feature of the educational arena is the degree to which so many people are aware of the political and social dynamics that transpire around them. There is, for example, the story of a young man who, by the time he was fifteen, was as active in community politics as anyone could ever be, but who now at the time of entering college is already retreating from the narcissistic boasts of his own leaders. This young man once sought help from Chicano leaders in his efforts to increase the visibility of Chicano culture in a local high school and library. But the leaders betrayed him, using him as a stepping-stone, he believes. And so, as he commences college, he appears ready to be a member of UMAS, but not a part of "any movement that uses hatred to fight hatred."

The story of this Adams State freshman is an important one, for none of us must believe that any political movement possesses a consistent ideology, or that all of those who claim to be a part of a movement honor it equally through their passions and commitments. Personal aggrandizement and selfish power permeate all units of the infamous political spectrum, and, like it or not, those of us involved in educational institutions are part of a politically charged world, and thereby remain susceptible to whatever it is that afflicts or enhances that world. To be sure, the sounds of the educational environment, like the home environment, are usually the sounds of the young; their squeals of delight, their fears, their inconsolable sobbing or pledges of revenge when an adult turns his back upon them. But schools, like homes, are run by adults themselves constrained and directed by other adults, or by young people drinking in adulthood and the so-called proper way as fast as they can. An Adams State referendum proposed by UMAS to collect a fee of two dollars per quarter from each student for scholarships was passed but then declared invalid by the president of A.S. & F. Pat Manchester declared the referendum of May 28 and 29, 1971, to be null and void. His announcement indicated that the ballot was not approved by the A.S. & F. council, that there was no publicity, and that the fee and associated constitutional changes were misrepresented.

It all comes to form the predicament that educational institutions everywhere now confront, a predicament that matters even to those who do not know a single Mexican-American child or who have in our schools a tiny and "well-behaved" group of black youngsters. It is in the lives of the people, in their histories, in their language (or languages), and not just in the rhetoric of their leaders or in the lessons of their teachers that we learn what recent social and political movements mean. The way people lead their lives and speak about these lives, even to visitors, is proof of their need for democracy and the chance to survive protected by rather than constrained by laws, economics, social regulations, and forms of government. Almost every family I have ever visited in what I regularly call my research looks to the child-care center, the neighborhood school, the college nearby or far away as *the* place for democracy to play itself out. "School will give my child the chance I never could give him," a woman in Alamosa told me. "They are good people in that school, and they know what is right for my child, for all our children as a matter of fact. Yours too. If he doesn't pass his courses, he doesn't deserve to have a responsible place in our community."

Millions of us in this country feel precisely the way this mother does, even to the extent that we may abdicate our own influences on our children and let the teachers and administrators take care of everything. But now there are also millions of people who, having seen the insides of schools, feel that the democracy offered by these schools can be no better than that offered by the nation itself. And some cannot even find the money to pay for the costs of college admissions tests. They feel betrayed and hurt, believing themselves to be systematically disenfranchised, stripped of their rights. They feel angry or foolish, too, because their needs are so different from the needs and purposes of those well established in schools and in the nation. As ironic as it seems, some are by their seventeenth birthday disillusioned both with the society and the political leaders, even the revolutionaries claiming to know ways to make things better. And some feel ashamed because education has been good to them but not to their brothers and sisters whom they now will "leave behind" as markers of their own advancement. Every day, pride, shame, self-consciousness, achievement, knowledge, and revolution undergo redefinitions; and with these realities go others like curriculum reform, classroom behavior, course requirements, academic majors, and relevance. As the concepts of education are redefined, and as the students yell or battle or come to be quiet again, and as their elders immerse themselves in one crisis after another or run away from the crises and the rhetoric and the rage they cannot at this time tolerate or reconcile with their work, human beings evolve.

There is something simple and poetic about this fact, something that underlies the Chicano Movement, all the movements: Knowledge grows; educational organizations and technologies reach capacities and levels of complexity no one anymore can untangle. But right with them, as quiet shadows, linger the same old wretched illnesses that America has always known: hunger, human deprivation, disease, lack of political representation, and all varieties of doors and gates and walls that keep certain people from sharing a present and a future that so many of the rest of us can rely on. Schools are a part of this. What is more, what scintillates in the lives of minority group people I have spoken with and, indeed, grown up with, is a need to repossess and nurture a tradition, a cultural inheritance, a place, and a past — the very need that often is disparaged or denied by a society that demands assimilation and commonality. Schools are a part of this too. The new words, like *Chicano, Chicanismo, El Movimiento,* and the new people who honor these words have not yet been accepted by some of us innkeepers of education who feel the ground moving beneath us and a certain intellectual history we once believed to be so right and logical slipping away from our reach. Can we then, I wonder, fully appreciate the message from Jesús Chavarría when he writes in one of the languages of his culture: "What we mean by education and what we mean by Chicano Studies is *freedom.*"